Poems from *Thrown Again into the Frazzle Machine*:

About "Beginning a Very Long List"
"Beautiful...may very well be my favorite poem ever!"
MaryAnn Myers

About "My Own Tribute"
"I saw Pete Seeger a long time ago when he sailed into Marblehead Harbor and gave a concert - such a great man - you captured his essence so beautifully...."
Ruth Estrich

About "Sarah Horn Sings with Kristen Chenoweth":

"I can relate to every word...Beautiful poem."
Sarah Horn

"Every word just resonates with universal truth. This is what happens when art, creativity and a willingness to (as you eloquently say) open the heart converge."
Marsha L. Browne

About "Portrait of Michael Smith":

"Thank you, Margaret. I love the poem."
Michael Smith

"Your poem is very lovely and perceptive. I've known Michael for over 35 years and watched him grow and mature as an artist and person. I think your poem captures that."
Rich Warren

THROWN AGAIN
INTO THE
FRAZZLE MACHINE

Also by Margaret Dubay Mikus

BOOKS:
As Easy as Breathing: Reclaiming Power for Healing and Transformation—Poems, Letters and Inner Listening

Letting Go and New Beginnings: A Mother's Poetic Journey

CHAPBOOK:
New Year's Eve Surgery

CD:
Full Blooming: Selections from a Poetic Journal

CARDS:
Life Support Cards ™

THROWN AGAIN
INTO THE
FRAZZLE MACHINE

Poems of Grace, Hope and Healing

Margaret Dubay Mikus, Ph.D.

Thrown Again into the Frazzle Machine:
Poems of Grace, Hope, and Healing

Copyright © 2015 by Margaret Dubay Mikus

Published by Margaret Dubay Mikus
at *Three Heart Press*

Printed by CreateSpace

ISBN: 0692344055 (pbk)
ISBN-13: 978-0692344057 (pbk)

Also available as an E-book with full color photos

All rights reserved.
No part of this book may be reproduced or transmitted in any form or by any means. Written permission from the copyright holder is required for use of any part of this book including poems, photographs, and prose, except in the case of brief quotations in critical articles and reviews.

www.FullBlooming.com

Front cover photo by Margaret Dubay Mikus
Cover design by Margaret Dubay Mikus and Donna Casey
(www.DigitalDonna.com)
Author photo by Stephen Mikus

Thank you to the editors who chose these poems for previous publication:

In *Journal of Modern Poetry* (JOMP), editor CJ Laity
JOMP 16, 2013: "Floating On Sitar Notes and Drum Beats" and "Just Before Tops Diner." *JOMP 17*, 2014: "Towards the End"

In *Willow Review*, 2013, editor Michael Latza
"Loving Detachment," "Meltdown," "Put Down the Sword of Self-Wounding," "This Big Thing," "From the Stars," "Because My Star," "Room on Cardiology Floor," "Reconsider," "What Is Important," "The Leaving of It," "Side by Side," "Healing Grief," "Poetry Reader: The Times We Are In," "Good Week: For Amy," "Somewhere in the Middle More Towards the End," "Past Dusk Walk"

In *Spirit Imprints* magazine, 2012, editor, Pramod Uday
"Grieving as Part of Life," "The Signature" and "From Eric, Prada, Crystal, and Others"

In *Letting Go and New Beginnings: A Mother's Poetic Journey*, 2011, by Margaret Dubay Mikus, Ph.D.
"Loving Detachment," "This Big Thing," "From Mary Jane D. and Stephenie Meyer," "Not Easy," "Melting," "You Can Ask," "My Daughter," "Ankles Cracking on the Stairs" and "Escape Velocity"

LincolnshireYoga.com (Bruce Symonds, teacher): "True Yoga"

In *Inspiring Story* in Belleruth Naparstek's blog, October, 2009 (**healthjourneys.com**): "From the Stars"

Many poems first appeared on my blog, (originally *Space of Grace*, incorporated into the re-design of FullBlooming.com in 2013). All blog posts are at www.fullblooming.com/blog

*For Stephen, who lived this with me,
together through thick and thin*

8/23/06

Loving Detachment

To love and let go
even more so...yes

no result in mind
not even safety.

I do not know
why you came

but I do know
there is reason

behind apparent madness,
seeds of growth

sown in bog of darkness,
inevitable love infuses chaos.

Life is messy and rich
and unexpected.

Even funny...
yes.

Contents

Loving Detachment xi

In Gratitude 1

Introduction 3

2009

For Lisa D'E 9
Meltdown 11
Caused to Stop and Think 13
Floating On Sitar Notes and Drum Beats 14
For B.R....Again 16
New Hole 17
One Day When I Am Gone 18
Knowing What I Know Would I Let You Go? 19
Inspired by Something Partly Heard on the Radio 20
Driving I-55 21
Put Down the Sword of Self-Wounding 22
The Crack Between 24
Scene: The Future 24
Remodeling as a Transformative Device 25
Pam 28
For John 30
The Answer 31
This Big Thing 32
From the Stars 34
Collagen 36
From Mary Jane D. and Stephenie Meyer 38
Not Easy 39
Melting 41
Plea for Tolerance 43
Burning the Candle at Both Ends 45
You Can Ask 46

My Daughter   46
Purpose?   47
Ankles Cracking on the Stairs   48
Mirror: For Jan Gerber   49
Thanksgiving Grieving   51
Soon Enough   54
Animals on the Journey Home   55
Here I Am   56
Perfectly Imperfect   57
Where We Are in the Story   58
An Accounting   60
How to Not Feel a Failure   61
A Way to Release Sorrow   63
Small Hope   65

2010

Soave   69
Flying Geese   70
Because My Star   71
Selective Memory   72
Something Small   73
Ask and Response   75
Speaking Kidney   76
Family Photo   77

2010, Surgery

Complications   81
Comfort   82
Consternation   83
Hold On   84
Beginning a Very Long List   86
Room on Cardiology Floor   88
Gratitude   89
How I Choose to Tell the Story   90
Post Surgery Follow-Up   91
Deer   92

Inspired   93
Recipe   94
If I Had Known   95
Mustering Illusive Understanding   96
Close from a Distance   97
Life Skill   98
The Rest of the Story...   99
Attitude   100
Dear Body   100

2010, Life Resumes

Aftertaste   103
Reconsider   104
Ultimately Hopeful Witness   105
Left Wanting   106
Shadow Healing   107
Escape Velocity   110
Convert the Pain   111
Not Exactly Recrimination   112
Sitting With It   113
To Err on the Side of Caution   115
Real Cactus   116
Yes, I Noticed You Being You   117
Doors (3)   118
Thinking of You   120
Lie Down   121
Someone Said   122
Saturday Morning   123
Suggestible from a Distance   124
Memorial to a Joyful Life   126
The Mechanics of Healing   128
What I Saw   129
Affirming   130
For Lisa and Me   131
Not Exactly a Memoir   132
Dodge Poetry Festival #5   134
When You Left a Hole to Fill   135
Dodge Poetry Festival #11   137

Book Signing: Kay Ryan   138
Just Before Tops Diner   139
Reaction   141
The Day After the Call   142
Prayer for My Youngest Brother   143
At Odds   144
For Robert Pattinson   145
What Is Important   146
Right in Front of Me   147
Emotional Control   148
Reading *The Cruelest Month* by Louise Penny   150
For Alex In Times of Trouble   151
Inevitable Woman Nature?   153
The Leaving of It   154

2011

Waiting in Michigan   157
For Stephen   159
Side by Side   160
Healing Grief   161
After   162
Poetry Reader: The Times We Are In   162
Traveling   163
From the 31st Floor at the Hyatt   164
For Rae   165
Hanging On   166
Mom   167
In Recovery   168
Mom Back in Hospital   169
Mom Report   170
Rae's Last Day   171
Early Days   172
Before/After Dr. Lisa   174
Remember Japan   176
Basking in Solitude   177
Deep Grieving   178
Casual Witness   179
Stretching Scars   179

Good Week: For Amy   180
Watching Boats on the Lake   181
For My Mother   183
Ten Days Left— Give or Take   184
Grieving as Part of Life   185
Strength   187
An Ordinary Conversation   189
Road Kill   190
Sniping   191
True Yoga   192
Hard Fall   193
Considering   196
The Greater Tuberosity   197
Follow-Up, Dr. Jason K.   198
To Hammer   200
Returning to the Scene   202
For Barbara and Me In Some Ways in the Same Boat   203
Abrupt Clarity   205
Startling Starlings   207
Intoxication of Hope   208

2012

Remembering a Little Girl   211
If Then Yes   212
The Signature   213
Waiting at the Mini Car Repair   214
To Welcome the New   215
Choosing Expansive   217
Inspired   218
Monday Call   219
Broken Shoulder   220
Somewhere in the Middle More Towards the End   222
Baby Robins   223
In the Rain: Randolph St., Chicago   224
Reborn at 60   225
Monday Conversation   227
Being   227
From Eric, Prada, Crystal, and Others   228

Living in the Present Tense   229
The Penultimate Visit   231
After Kip (No Singing)   234
The Children Are Watching   235
Cactus Flower   236
7/13/12 AM   237
Gratitude as an Antidote to Grief   238
Grief and the Heart   239
Gorecki: Symphony of Sorrowful Songs   240
Jean McGrew Crosses the Bridge   242
Medication   244
Reading *Garment of Shadows* by Laurie R. King   245
For STM   246
Those Times   247
Three Months Out   248
Evening Walk   250
Grief Report—Four Months Out   251
Another Sister with Cancer   252
Permission to Myself   253
Evening Walk   254
Sliced by a Mandoline   255
Past Dusk Walk   256

2013

For My Son Who Is Leaving   259
Evening Walk Series   260
Walking Series: January Thaw   261
John is Dying They Say   262
Trusting I Will Know   263
Saturday Walk 5PM   264
Wake for My Brother   265
1964-2013   266
Prayer of Intercession   267
Funeral Night   268
Finished Later   269
Resolution of Darkness   270
Momentary   271
Appearance Can Deceive   272

Grief-Stricken   273
Metastases   273
From Jerry De G   274
Saturday Backyard   275
Thinking of Dorothy   276
The House on Cadieux   278
Stronger than You Think   279
Too Many Shoes   280
For My Baby Sister   281
Return   282
Take Care   283
Grateful   284
Phone Calls after Voice Lessons   285
Coming to Terms   287
Written at the Bahia Resort   288
Fear of Relaxation   289
For Comfort, Really   290
First Egret of the Season   291
Hope and Directions   292
Heart Instructions/Description   294
To Unravel Mystery   296
Not Looking Ahead Exactly   297
Nearing Anniversary   298
Yesterday's Walk   300
Bedroom Window   301
Antidote to Violence   302
My Love,   303
Singer with the Rough Voice   304
Aggressor   305
Daily Pattern   306
The Other Side of Rain   307
Not Up to Me   309
Summer Night   310
MRI on Wed.   311
Almost 1 Year Later   312
Virtual Choir 4   313
Listening to and Reading Neil Gaiman   315
29th Birthday   316
Moving Closer   317

Shooting Stars   319
Good Books   321
Sarah Horn Sings with Kristin Chenoweth   322
Eric Whitacre: *Godzilla Eats Las Vegas*   324
Fearless in the Face of Panic   325
Glass Blowing   326
Sitting for a Portrait   327
Few Days Ago   328
Vacation   320
4 AM   330
Mom's Birthday   331
After Talking with Dorothy   332
One Moment, Then the Next   334
The Path   335
Resilience   336
Helicopter   337
For Kelly's Mom   338
Emotional Stew   339
Considering Mortality and Beyond   341
Walking Series   342
To Lift Sorrow Out   343
Preparing for Echocardiogram   344
Towards the End   345
Changes Everything   346
Dreaming of Dance   347
The Joke   349
After Roberta Who Asked   350

2013, Surgery
Healing through Re-Writing the Old Story

ER 2AM   353
Little Sister   355
Cockeyed   356
Observing Geese   357
Awareness   358
From Inside   359
Uterus 1   360
New Doctors   361

To Trust Again?   363
Another New Surgeon   364
To Tell You   365
Safe and Spooned   366
Kinds of Anxiety   367
Uterus 2   368
Rewind: Senseless Tragedy   370
Shadow and Sun   373
Still Thinking of Victor   374
Faith   375
White Woman from Illinois on Mandela   376
Dear Uterus: 378
Back to a Single Surgery   380
Addendum to the Life List   381
Post-Surgery   382
Thrown Again into the Frazzle Machine   383
A Tiny Bit   384
Dodged a Bullet   385
Partnership   387
Accomplishment   389
All Is Well   389
Mother   390
Cervix   392
Effects of Anesthesia   393
From the Perspective of the Tree   395
Home from the Hospital   396
Loss   397
Energy Restored   398

2014, Post-Surgery, Life Resuming

Another Serious Diagnosis   403
First Night   403
May Be Called New Year   404
Door Into   405
History of the Hernia   406
Fact of the Matter   410
Snow   411
Changing Rules   412

Continual Conundrum   414
Vanished   415
Portrait of Michael Smith   416
Awareness of Progress   417
For Midge and Me   418
Non-Surgical Solutions   419
Ready to Be Released Back into the Wild   420
Six-Week Follow-Up   421
On Imperfection: For Corax   423
My Own Tribute   424
Still Fragile   426
Conscious   426
Reflection   427
Alok the Doctor   429
To Affirm   430
At Home in the Universe   431
Amidst the Buzz   432
Ripple Effect   434
Under the Influence   435
Melt   435
This Night   436
Full in It   436
Metamorphosis of Water   437
Empress of Inertia   438
West Yard   439
Red Fox   439
Seven Deer at Dusk   440
Metaphor for What?   441
Sturgeon Bay   442
Familiar Dark   443
Another Crisis   445
Office Thaw-Fly   446
Routine Checkup   447
Learning to Listen   448
2% 5-Year Survival Rate   449
Someone Posted on Facebook   450
1980s at a Guess   451
Threadbare   452
Melt Gift   452

In the Dark Mist of the Past   453
Dear Wednesday: 454
Noticing Owls   456
To Answer a Question Unstated   457
Global Reach   459
Approaching 40 Yrs. Married   460
Controlled Burn   461
Snow In April   462
Self-Kindness   463

Timeline   464

Notes: Poems   466

Notes: Photos   472

About the Author   474

Cast Off and Landing (photo)   476

In Gratitude

Flow of physical, mental, emotional, and spiritual energy is essential for creativity. I am more grateful than I can express for my personal healing team, especially: Barbara Racioppo, Ph.D. (clinical psychologist), Kip Snyder (voice teacher and more), Lisa D'Eramo, DC (holistic doctor), Katie Summers, MSAc (acupuncturist), Roberta Leenhouts, RN (EnergyTouch® practitioner) Crystal Simmons, LMT (therapeutic massage), Midge Heurich (Reiki), Alok Pant, MD (gynecological surgeon), Mohammad Waseem Kagzi, MD (internal medicine), Mehran Jabbarzadeh, MD (heart rhythm specialist), and Jason Koh, MD (orthopedic and sports medicine). For the surgery in 2013: Melissa Pant, MD (anesthesiologist), "my" ER crew at Advocate Condell Medical Center, including the ultrasound tech who was so kind, and my Lake Forest Hospital team, particularly Rosemary, the nurse-anesthetist who let me lean my (very heavy) head on her shoulder when the epidural had to be redone just after surgery.

Additionally, from earlier: Geary Davis, LAc (acupuncturist, light therapy and healing energy), Brigitte Bernold (therapeutic massage, Reiki, and yoga teacher), Tricia Eldridge (EnergyTouch® founder and practitioner), Frani Rubens, MS (healing energy sessions), Susi Roos, RN, MDiv (massage, Energetic Life Balancing, and healing energy sessions), Barbara Woolf and Bruce Symonds (yoga teachers), and Marilyn Mitchell, MD (women's health). Thank you to all!

I am immensely grateful for my loving family and friends, in times of crisis and also joy: Stephen Mikus, Alex Mikus, Blake Mikus, Evan Johnson, Dorothy Sobota, Marie Smith, Tom Dubay, Barbara Nealon, Mary Anne Mikus, Chris and Llubav Duerr, Dorothy Calpin, Virginia Dubay Post, Rae and Ted Mikus, Karen Baker, and Lena Dobbs-Johnson.

Overflowing with gratitude to early readers and listeners who encouraged me to complete this collection. Their positive voices in my head ("Velcro sentences") helped me overcome discouragement: Kip Snyder, Crystal Simmons, Midge Heurich, Stephen Mikus, Dorothy Sobota, and Roberta Leenhouts.

I am grateful for my collaboration with Donna Casey (graphic designer) to complete the beautiful cover. Alex Mikus provided invaluable editing and proof reading. Her meticulous care, enthusiasm, and thoughtful reading made this a better book. Working with her was a true gift. Thank you so much!

Connecting with friends from the International Women's Writing Guild inspired and supported me, especially Amy Temple, MaryAnn Myers, Pam Frost, Anne Schneider, and Marj Hahn. I am grateful for the generous encouragement of Pramod Uday. Her gentle kindness, from across the globe, meant a great deal to me.

Heartfelt thanks to Elizabeth Gilbert, Oriah Mountain Dreamer, Anne Lamott, Louise Penny, and Neil Gaiman. Their writing and speaking consistently urged me to speak my truth in my own worthy voice, continuing to make good art from my life, and then to have courage and let it go. And to Eric Whitacre who created in Virtual Choir a global community of incredibly supportive singers (without boundaries). His stunning music moves the heart and heals the soul. He continues to inspire me and meeting him was profoundly moving.

Thank you, Barbara Mertz (aka Elizabeth Peters), 1927-2013. Reading her entire Amelia Peabody series was a comfort to me many times over the years as I was healing from serious illness or escaping from darkness. When I wrote to tell her, she graciously replied with a handwritten note (which I framed).

Finally, I am most deeply grateful to all who have inspired me over the years. These poems would not exist and I would not be the same without you.

Introduction

May these poems and photographs be a lifeboat through hard times for you or someone you know. Perhaps this book will give comfort, healing, and hopefulness. Although this is a very personal story, aspects might seem familiar to you, might give voice to something in your life, express something you want to say, or be a way to help someone you care about. I should tell you right off it has a very happy ending as I came through what seemed like a long black tunnel, "the only way out, is through...."

For this collection I selected poems from 2009 through April of 2014. This was a particularly "rough patch" with losses piling on and additional serious medical problems, (interspersed with walks, people, music, reflection, and calm insights). The poems are a record of that time, a way to process, assess, and remember, both at the time and later. Originally I wanted to tell the story of two surgeries (in 2010 and 2013), how the second surgery helped to heal trauma from the previous one. I then added some poems to give context and flesh out the story. The book kept evolving, getting bigger for a while, some poems in, some poems out, until it coalesced over time into this volume.

Although I think of myself as a strong and vigorous person, my whole life I've struggled with various health issues. In 1995 I healed from multiple sclerosis, setting out on a new life course. My creativity was cracked open and I began a poetic journal to "sing from the heart." Within a year, a diagnosis of breast cancer threw me into a whirlwind of emotions and medical treatment decisions. With help, I integrated holistic and conventional therapies and healed from cancer. Those insights led to my first book, *As Easy as Breathing: Reclaiming Power for Healing and Transformation—Poems, Letters and Inner Listening.* Writing continues to be essential to me for a healthy and meaningful life.

Three broad take-home messages of this book are: 1) Healing, insight, and growth can take place all the time, on the most ordinary days. Poems like "Put Down the Sword of Self-Wounding," "Remodeling as a Transformative Device," "Melting," and "Convert the Pain" speak to transformation as a process that transcends painful experiences. It may not be about going off on retreat, away from the complexity of life, but in persisting day to day through even the messiest crazy times. Slowly you might become aware of what needs healing, begin to ask for help and to receive it, learn new skills, and remember what you already know about taking good care of yourself. 2) Healing is possible even after waves of grief or illness or other traumas keep knocking you down until you can no longer remember anything but darkness. Crucial ingredients for me were grace, persistence, trust, patience, inner guidance, putting one foot in front of the other day after day, writing, being in nature, drawing support to me, remembering to breathe, practicing radical self-care and self-kindness. 3) It is possible to heal by "re-writing the old story," not to change what happened in the wounded past, but to change the conclusion. Poems tell of a major surgery gone wrong in 2010 and then another surgery in 2013 that was healing in every way possible. The first surgery was traumatic to remember and so I wrote very little, and the second I wanted to recall every detail. By re-writing the old story, the surgery in 2013 led to a restoration of hope and trust, and profound healing of body, mind, emotion, and spirit.

Change is possible. Healing is possible. It is possible to heal our whole selves, to heal relationships, to heal our severed connection to our life purpose, and to heal trauma, whatever the cause. We can heal our past and set a new course for ourselves free from old ingrained injuries. If one person heals, healing energy radiates out from them with the possibility of healing their families and communities. We all benefit as it spills over to all of us.

These small slices of life from my poetic journal share a hopeful story. Various threads are woven over time into a narrative arc: ongoing medical events, my longtime deep connection to my husband, the closeness of our family of four, celebrating my relationship with my mother through poems inspired by our Monday phone calls, then grieving her loss and also that of my youngest brother, my father-in-law and mother-in-law, and many other close family members and friends (see Timeline). My youngest sister, Dorothy, was diagnosed with aggressive stage 4 breast cancer. The disappearance of a friend of my daughter (a girl who used to sit on a stool at my kitchen counter) profoundly affected me as a mother ("For Kelly's Mom" and "Vanished"). I selectively read and responded to the news. Many people inspired me, many people helped me. I am truly grateful. The "Walking Series" poems are peaceful meditations of being present in nature. When I was pulled more into the medical realm, the poems more narrowly focused on that world. As I emerged from an intensive healing period, the poems became more wide-ranging again.

Even in the hardest times, not every minute is relentless, conscious healing work. Sometimes you need a vacation from grief, a respite in nature, a good laugh, a nap, a walk, a book, singing, a silly movie, talking with a friend about anything else, some sliver of perspective. Something to feel normal, to remember that there is life apart from all the dark, a life you can move towards—in zigs and zags—as the days go on.

So take this lifeboat with me through some rough seas and calm, into the streaming light on the far shore. Let me tell you a story...

September 16, 2014

Margaret Dubay Mikus

2009

1/29/09

For Lisa D'E
After Sharon Olds

Does it matter why
a half bowling ball
sticks out from my middle?

Do I need to know
the when and the how and the who
did what to whom?

And if I suck it in,
it does not move
as if unattached to muscle

untethered from nerve.
Many possibilities,
all plausible.

But I am not a victim,
angry, sad, or complaining.
I am a pilgrim

who no longer seeks,
who is content breathing,
considering the possibilities.

A joyful and generous soul
who has been subjected to…
who has repeatedly had

unwarned long-term effects—
oh, if I had only known,
would I have chosen otherwise?

Maybe not....
The path is laid out
and a feather is enough,

the slightest breath of wind enough,
to shift my course
to alignment.

2/4/09

Meltdown

To melt,
to be liquefied
under high heat.

To go down,
to fall,
to not be rising.

To change the state of matter,
to become more dispersed,
to become both more and less.

To lose emotional control,
to weep unceasingly,
to seek higher ground

and not find.
To float lost
as if it would always be thus.

To release,
to let go the anchor,
to be unwilling to jump

and yet jump
or be pushed
by dire circumstance.

To come out the other side
of this trial by fire,
to know it would always

end this way.
To be cleansed,
to re-form,

to cool and coalesce,
altered, yet beautiful,
even luminescent.

2/6/09

Caused to Stop and Think

*Woman at fitness club lying on gurney
in an office behind glass walls,
heart rate 200 and won't come down.
Ambulance and fire truck outside, lights flashing.*

When I drop in my tracks
there will still be work to be done,
stains I haven't removed,
loose buttons I have not re-sewn.

There will still be mail to be sorted,
bills to be paid, emails and calls returned.
Poems will remain even more unwritten,
perhaps someone else will make the daily bed.

Some things will go undone,
even important things
will be important to no one.
What will remain of all the days' labors

is the love I have received and given,
what healing was accomplished,
what beauty I made
and what I have already written.

2/14/09

Floating On Sitar Notes and Drum Beats
Dinner at The Peacock *on Valentine's*

So much done to the body.
So much stored in the body.

The body a map of the past,
the snake entwined around Eve.

The body: the sitar, the lotus, the onion,
the pond to swim in, and the fish swimming.

The foam in the cup,
the gyrations of dance,

the main course,
not so much dessert.

The color red as it
plays on the water,

the helium balloon,
the red rubber ball,

the accelerating rhythm,
the glint on sheer glass,

baby's breath and
tiny ruby carnations.

It is amplified,
it is sober and still,

plays well with others,
puts dirty feet on the table.

The body is the flying horse,
the sparkle on new snow,

it is a glass full
and a glass empty.

It is payment for services,
it is the nourishment taken in,

it is the pen and the words
and the hopefulness.

It is less like soap
and more like anise seeds,

more a home, than a prison.

2/25/09

For B.R....Again

She said one line
that changed everything,

one true sentence easily uttered
illuminating a dark path

I had not been able to alter.
Exact words did not stick

but the gist was this:
when I had a good energy day

I did not trust it to last
to the next.

I stayed up late with
all my pent up desire

mortgaging each following day
sabotaging my future.

Trust. So simple a lesson.
Go to bed and trust

the sun will rise the next morning.
Not exactly that simple but close.

Use up in one day
only what is for that day.

Rest. Incorporate. Percolate.
Wait and see what will show up

unexpectedly.

3/3/09

New Hole

If it were you
having to push back in
through an unnatural hole
the guts that inevitably come through
could you do it?

Even in discussion
grimace in reaction
to description of the action,
taking fingers with trimmed nails
and push until concave abdomen.

Let go. Later, again. And again...
Usually not painful
but if stuck outside,
unbearable.
Two surgeries,

recovery upon recovery.
Again a new hole
bigger, in a new place.
Why trust what has not worked?

3/24/09

One Day When I Am Gone

the ruffled waters will calm.
One day when I am gone

not the first day I suspect
the sky will be ordinary blue

and the stars will shine true
not as through tears

and the hole that might have been
will be filled except for a few bad days

as if the ocean had risen
to fill a hole in the sand.

One day I will be gone
yet you may think of me still

remembering how it all began
seeing the long arc of the story

the inevitable end.

The end that is the beginning...
trust me.

4/3/09

Knowing What I Know Would I Let You Go?

For Aunt Marlene and Uncle Tom

If the time came
would I be able to
give you up

my friend, my soulmate
my heart
knowing we have been together

over and over
trusting we would be together
always?

No, I think not
I would fight for you
to stay with me

I would rage at the Universe
I would thrash and struggle
until...

4/26/09

Inspired by Something Partly Heard on the Radio

I do not know
how much time
I have with you.

I read the stories—
or avoid reading them—
of all the sad, tragic

things that happen
and tears run down my face
in sympathy, in empathy

whether I would stop them
or not. I know this dark place.
Yet I do not

want to know the limits
of the hours, the minutes
I have with you.

What good would that do?
Just to be here
where you are

for as long
as there is...
and be grateful.

5/15/09

Driving I-55

Sun-shimmer ponds flood
unplowed fields of un-corn.

No birds.
No green fringe

or maybe one or two
a small patch here and there.

Motion-shadow of
truck filled to full.

White clapboards
nested in mature trees.

Horses as distant silhouettes
cows graze lush grass strips.

Half dome sky
bigger than anything.

Some houses intact
some buildings crumbling.

Hard to say or see
what might be thriving.

The sun shines
after torrential rains

it is spring
on the Illinois plains.

5/28/09

Put Down the Sword of Self-Wounding
After talking to Geary about a ritual to ease pain

Put down the sword
of self-destruction
and self-immolation,

of self-defeat, self-demolition,
and self-defacing. Stop
stabbing myself in the vulnerable gut

in remorse, guilt, grief and regret
at what I could not
control or plan or shape.

Melt that sword
into the ploughshare
that carves the furrows

into which I place
the seeds I have been holding back.
Let forgiveness

flood the field,
let love shine upon them,
let the earth be fertile and loam-rich

and bountiful harvest my just reward.
After all the lifetimes
of all the dark and light alike

let my new life
result from a conscious new choice:
to put down the sword.

No more self-blame
self-criticism or self-judging,
no more crimson shame,

no more self-harsh words,
no more self-unkindness,
no more self-disrespect,

or screaming at myself
at perceived imperfections
or unbearable failings.

Only forgiveness
to the bone of things
to the bottom and top of memory,

forgiveness heaped
on forgiveness, eaten
at a great feast of forgiveness.

And when sated,
love as dessert and
as the main course ever after.

8/2/09

The Crack Between

A poem
tucked in the crack

between breakfast toast
and washing dishes

some words insist
on being written.

8/19/09

Scene: The Future

Ten years from now
they will look
at my exceeding flat chest—
irregular peaks razed to sea level—

shake their heads and say:
we would never do that now
over such slight provocation.
But we live in the time we live,
choose from the proffered menu of choices

as best we can, with whatever guidance
we can muster and absorb,
whatever hopefulness we can bear,
not knowing if anything else will come.

9/5/09

Remodeling as a Transformative Device (Better than Illness)

Every summer for a long time,
or often anyway,
illness has caught me—
serious enough to warrant
immediate concern,
life-threatening even.

All time was then divided
into before the diagnosis
and after it, life wiped
away as I had known it,
what had seemed important
became less than trivial.

Amnesia set in
about how things had been
and I couldn't get back
to "normal."
The process of healing
took the time it took

and the lessons came
and some stuck,
some left until
the next time.
On and on it went
with help coming at key moments.

I learned how to ask and receive.
I learned how to balance in chaos.
How to laugh at darkness.
How to let myself feel
and even cry in the presence of others.

And I wrote it all down:

the insights, the quest, the stories
that seemed to give meaning
to suffering, to healing.
Was there no other way
to transformation than
ripping off my skin
again and again?

Then, this summer:
remodeling—let everything be different
than it had been. Let clutter
be cleared, past failures forgiven,
all belongings spread out,
nothing where it had been.

Ask: If I were moving,
would I keep this?
As dusty carpet went out
and clean wood floors went in,
light came too, gleaming.
Kitchen cabinets refaced in rich cherry,

Santa Cecelia (patron saint of creativity)
was the name of our chosen granite from Brazil.
All that was worn and shabby
made new again.
Moving on without moving away.
Color, space, clean air,

promise, possibility, openness.
We can't find our way back
to what was...
even if we wanted to.
Old habits are breaking:
like how high to reach to answer the phone

or where are a pair of scissors or stamp or fork,
little is where it was,
all part of the 17 or 39 or whatever number
of changes in the environment to sustain
healing changes in me.

And the rest of the family?
Well, they are in the thick and thin of it too.
If they can be nourished by all this,
if they can learn to function
without the usual foundation,

if they can be surrounded by and
immersed in energy for where they are going...
all the better.

9/6/09

Pam

She showed up at my door
at one of my darkest hours
with large, chilled, fresh aloe leaves

and a potted aloe plant.
She was a yoga friend, an angel of mercy
come to take care of me.

I was deep burned from radiation,
you could feel the heat
across a large room,

and the marks were three hearts:
two, dark red flanking my neck,
one, inverted white at my throat.

I wasn't the only one
who could see them.
I could not bear even clothes.

She moved away soon after
and we lost touch.
She might have emailed,

and I might have seen her once
years later at another table
in a nearby pizza place.

Her aloe gift plant outgrew the pot,
was cut back, repotted, and wildly grew again.
Years have passed and now that gift

from her hands on my front porch,
is scraggy and unwieldy.
Time to go you know, time to go.

Time to let go of the memory even
of all that happened
the first time cancer came knocking.

9/20/09

For John

You asked a simple question
and inadvertently set in motion
a flood of memory.

How did we come to be here?
Now the choice seems clear,
the answer pat, in a way,

without the young agony
of lives stretching out to infinity,
having to choose a course,

knowing only
we would be together and
that was all that really mattered.

There were reasons
this was the place
all the ducks lined up.

But there was no road map,
no internet to search, no assurances,
we did our best to prepare

and then leapt.

9/22/09

The Answer

The hole in muscle-wall,
a symptom
of structural weakness,

current but not inherent,
not part of the original design
so elegantly carried out.

No, it was from living
and things happening
in 3 dimensions or 4 or more.

Choices were made and not made,
decisions set in motion,
and imperceptibly the erosion

of the under-layer, the core.
What once was built, can be re-built
that is not the question.

The answer of course
is yes.
Clearly changes are called for.

10/6/09

This Big Thing

If you knew how long
it would take to do
this big thing,
this vision,

you would never begin.

If you knew how much
energy at times,
how little sleep at times,
how many tiny details

would make up the whole,
what worries, what waiting,
what driving, what negotiation
what re-invention, what chaos

you would never begin.

You would not know how
the progress of day to day
could feed you,
awaken you, open doors for you,

let in light and space and room to breathe.
If you had not trusted,
if you did not understand clarity,
if you thought you were standing alone

you would never begin.

Or so it seems
about all the other times
big plans stalled,

and so it seems

looking back on the
peaceful revolution miracle of
allowing change to unfold,
even embracing.

From fearful to sure,
or sure enough
to take one step...
then another, not necessarily big leap.

Not to erase the past,
but creating the future, your future,
from the endless supply
of present moments.

10/12/09

From the Stars

Here I am
naked before you
all scars, weakness,
vulnerability revealed

as beautiful.

Steely resolve,
stubborn determination,
hard-won power

as foundation.

Unashamed,
unassuming,
hiding nothing
I might once have deemed

unacceptable.

Something to be said for
enduring, growing,
transforming, transcending.

Every wrinkle
tells a story
of care or neglect.

Every scar a tale
of chance or choice,
guilt, healing, awareness, or regret.

I can tell you
have come from the stars
just to see

life here in action.
Here I am.

10/15/09

Collagen

Making collagen
to heal from damage done
with the best intention.

Collagen
re-connecting again
what seems broken.

A hole in muscle
surrounded by weakness
that heals then gets worse.

Energy grid is in place,
fully intact not torn,
focused blue-light structural layer.

Protein to make collagen,
to see it as unbroken,
to feel and sense and know beyond belief.

If I am whole
will the writing stop,
will I cease to hear,

will I forget to pay attention?
What is the ancient deep-seated, fear-kernel
of being vibrantly healthy?

That expectation will be
a higher bar than I can reach?

That I will never rest
with so much energy flowing?

That health is like balance,
only momentarily attainable

and then will I fall prey
to the next shadow-lurking thing?

But back to collagen,
no miracle drug,

no wonder molecule
from without,

but a competent component
easily and often manufactured,

the glue, the foundation,
the lattice-lace upon which

I am truly re-born
already fully capable.

10/17/09

From Mary Jane D. and Stephenie Meyer
For Ira, Bob, Geary and Eric

Something that shatters
pre-existing life structure
stretching out to the foreseeable future.

No restoration
of equilibrium
or the familiar,

the details
don't matter:
a choice point where

all is divided into
before...and after
and darkness is the dominant color.

The decisive end...of what was,
the promising beginning...of what is:

verdant, vivid vibration,
riot of sensation,
vibrant colors of all description,

almost beyond bearing.

You get to the point
where you say: This
lightening bolt that struck me

was the best thing
that ever happened.

10/18/09

Not Easy

It has not been
an easy pregnancy
growing the new me.

Sometimes I have been sick
almost beyond bearing,
even despairing

the ordeal would never end.
And then the repeated
labor and deliveries…

I would not wish that
on anyone.
But the result…

yes, that is worth mentioning,
the new version that resulted
from the highest vision

I could have for myself
at any one time…
and the next and next…and on and on….

Yes, that was worth—
over and over again—
excruciating contractions.

And like in real life when
babies come and grow
and amnesia sets in,

and the focus shifts to the new desired vision,
if everything stayed perfectly fine,
would I still pay attention?

10/24/09

Melting

If you are willing
to melt
down to sinew and bones,

melt even muscle
hard-won
working to be fit.

(In its fibrous structure
muscle tissue traps
emotions ready for release.)

Melt even down to bone marrow,
primordial soup,
molecules ready to re-arrange.

All melted
and you are free,
I can tell you aren't yet happy.

This puddle of you,
this chrysalis,
this butterfly in the making,

in transition,
that familiar rough patch
neither here nor there.

But melt you must,
let rise to the top
what is worth saving

(what still serves you),
scoop it off
revel in the lightness of it,

of you.

Swallow, breathe,
re-build,
this time from cell-bricks

of purest love,
tempered in the oven
of life as it plays out,

stronger than anything
you could ever see, impervious
to sun, wind, quakes, and rain.

A miracle,
this new you,
worth a few months

of chaotic heat.
Patience rewarded,
trust repaid in full.

10/25/09

Plea for Tolerance
(If Not Whole-hearted Acceptance)

She was stunning—
a woman built upon
a male chassis—
gold leaves for hair,

slim body sheathed in
form-fitting gold brocade,
face sculpted from
coffee-cream marble.

The DJ was an incredible
exact replica of Edward Scissorhands,
power voice like Melissa Etheridge,
that could vibrate neurons,

stir submerged emotions,
bring unbidden tears to eyes
with the purity, intensity,
clarity, humanity of her song.

The nurse with long scarlet
pointed nails who shared her secrets,
a spicy woman residing in
an out-of-work carpenter's body,

a former altar boy,
affected by the downslide economy
who now used her time to help others—
build houses in New Orleans, teach,

walk for causes like AIDS and breast cancer,
a performer, a ready talker
once the key was found to her door.

The young newlyweds
comfortable in their openness,
invited their variegated friends
to their otherwise family-conventional

mid-summer wedding,
encouraging a female cousin
to dress as a man, upending
expected formal convention.

The costumed woman
in the school girl uniform
with the plaid miniskirt,
who had been a man

with diabetes,
had a kidney transplant
and everything, endured
up to seven shots daily

and then—through something,
some procedural removal,
some miracle—
was cured.

So many stories, voices longing
to be heard, lives to be witnessed,
searching for meaning, satisfaction, happiness...
just like all of us.

10/25/09

Burning the Candle at Both Ends

I am running out of candle
to burn at both ends

toward the ever-diminishing middle.
Take note.

Take action:
Stop and rest, my love.

Remember there are consequences,
remember the lessons learned

the hard way...
and pick easy.

10/29/09

You Can Ask

but I don't have to agree
to do a backward summersault
through multiple flaming hoops.

No longer need to please
anyone but myself
and that is a hard enough task

for a recovering perfectionist.

10/30/09

My Daughter

the full moon
and I am the tide
pulled inevitably
by her cycling

ebbing and flowing
with laws of nature
no conscious choice or intent
just females living together

in synchrony
one to the other
though I am always
and still, her mother

11/3/09

Purpose?

Uterus
denuded pear
still making known
its purpose

no longer birthing babies
shedding monthly detritus
but continual re-birthing of...
my Life

11/13/09

Ankles Cracking on the Stairs

Two grown children
though still young

embedded back into
the tapestry of days

like a journalist is
embedded on the front lines

like a YouTube video is
embedded on a blog or webpage

the code, part of the flow
making up the whole

and the removal—
inevitable really

for their life here
is not long—

their removal
will leave a hole...

again.
And again...the longing.

11/23/09

Mirror: For Jan Gerber

You are the seed crystal,
the often unsung hero,

the gatherer, the glue,
the creative spark,

the tranquil reflecting pool,
the gypsy fortune teller.

The one who risks,
the nurturer,

the shock absorber,
the way seeker,

the book maker,
the curator, the midwife,

creator of the grand design,
the one who keeps on.

The dreamer
and follower of the dream.

Trust, patience, truth,
good humor, good heart,

intelligence, hope,
inspiration, courage.

Listener, speaker,
avid student, natural teacher.

Persistent. Determined.
Enthusiastic. Resilient.

Kind and generous.
What of myself

is mirrored in you?

11/26/09

Thanksgiving Grieving

I can see him sitting there
so plainly on the kitchen chair,
cutting giblets for stuffing and gravy,
wanting help or company,

getting the big turkey ready
the night before the big day
so the oven could turn on
with the timer at maybe 5AM

and the bird was ready for
usual midday dinner on Sundays and holidays.
He also cooked the breakfast flat sheet

of scrambled eggs with maybe ham
or diced Canadian bacon, served with
sliced frosted cinnamon raison toast,
and reconstituted orange juice.

Those were his two cooking times
I remember, (well, also barbeques in summer)
Sunday after church, and Thanksgiving dinner.
Each year I see him still

though he's been gone now,
what is it—my son was almost a year,
and now he's 25—yes, that long.

Some years I feel dark
ahead of time, but this year
I was ambushed by grieving
as sharp as the first year.

Maybe with the remaining three parents
declining, their natural end
a matter of measured time.
Maybe it's the trip tomorrow to Michigan,

more usual for us after Christmas.
Maybe I feel vulnerable from being ill,
that skin-flayed unprotected feeling
of lacking normal intactness and strength.

Whatever it is
there it is:
I see him clearly

this complex, troubled man
this bear-hug-you,
turkey-cooking father

who once found a bike
someone had thrown out
and fixed the bent spokes
and the warped front wheel

and gave it to me
and I was glad of my very own two-wheeler.
And who would come get us

at some school game or dance.
Yes, there was the dark side,
the temper, the flash of built-up anger,

but today what I remember
is him looking up at me
from that Formica kitchen table

(big enough to seat nine of us)
in a house we no longer live in,
a man no longer living
except this one day in my fertile mind.

When anyone visiting would leave
he'd put on his jacket from the hook
at the back door, zip it up,
and wave them off,

the crunch of the gravel driveway.
When he'd leave, always the short toot! toot!
Except that last time....

11/27/09

Soon Enough

You seem to be cold
to my grieving

as if I could
plan my time to feel,

as if you did not
understand, but...

you have never faced
such circumstance.

And though I would not
wish this pain for you

it is part of life...
that it ends...

and loss too of loved ones
is part of life

as you will see soon enough,
my love.

11/27/09

Animals on the Journey Home

A hawk in flight,
red tail, full wing extension

lands on the bank
newly grass-sown and waits.

A raccoon curled up
by lanes of heavy traffic,

must be sleeping we used to say
to our small tender-heart children.

A deer on the highway lane line
recognizable only by bulk

of body and blood.
A dozen geese crossing

the hotel road at midnight.
We wait to let them pass.

12/15/09

Here I Am

Maybe if I am very still
and do not breathe (much)
or eat (much) or sleep (much)

the next wave of darkness
will miss me.
If I am very quiet and

do not attract attention—
is this making any sense?
(As if life made sense.)

From out there—or in there—
whichever is the vast velvet void,
I am sure all the pieces fit.

But I am here
frightened…some
trusting…some.

I am here, where it was chosen,
I am here in apparent duality,
I am here in apparent linear time

where hard things bob up
from the ocean of minutes and it could
be just innocuous clumps of seaweed

just brush off…or it could be
a landmine adrift, set off by casual touch.
How to know which is which?

12/16/09

Perfectly Imperfect

It is hard to be
out of sync with my body.
The body speaks and
I don't listen,

I try but
don't entirely succeed
to remember healing
is a process

begun somewhere else and
playing out in this dimension,
chaotic, messy, non-linear,
ungoverned by rational reason.

Begun and continued with good intention
some parts eager to hold
higher vibration,
some body parts slow or resistant.

Old business unfinished
rises to the surface,
balance and harmony elusive until…

a kind of forgiveness,
a wish for gentle kindness at least.

12/17/09

Where We Are in the Story

The blood is bright red
as a fresh wound

though dark clots indicate
some degree of age.

The top of the uterus is thick
as if just beginning to hold promise,

the bottom thinned to almost nothing
appropriate for her years.

What to say about this
top/bottom dichotomy,

duality manifest in
the pear-shape organ?

She was never reliable,
periods started early and stalled,

not once a month with the moon,
but a surprise now and then.

Later pills regulated the system
and bleeding came with the calendar.

Then two children
who came hard, not easy or gentle,

and other challenges:
frequent yeast infections

exacerbated by hormonal flux
and stress and antibiotics and....

Then chemo and stops.
Then re-start and stop bleeding again

at a better place in the cycle this time.
A dozen years pass and another cancer diagnosis,

choose to lose the ovaries to lessen risk.
 "Drips" and "spots" now and then,

and then this vast un-resolution.

12/17/09

An Accounting

I am not in pain
and that is a good thing.

I can breathe,
what a gift!

Some things are going on,
the life I have (at some point) chosen.

To remember to be
where I am at this moment,

to appreciate a warm loving body
lying next to me,

two healthy children
to love and be loved by.

What some would give
for any of this!

12/29/09

How to Not Feel a Failure

It is safe to say
I am sad about
how it all turned out.

Not sad as in
a momentary low,
but true and deep sorrow,

the more of it I let go
the more there is
to be released,

a dank swamp of emotion,
not redeeming perhaps,
no lifeboat I can grasp.

I am sinking
under the weight of it
and all the rest unfolding yet.

Voice gone,
my insides won't stay in,
and don't ask about digestion.

Self-image in tatters,
uterus confused, one half finished,
one half still expectant, as if

preparing to receive
a non-existent egg,
nourish a fetus phantom.

I am long done with all that,
the bleeding unwelcome,
the blatant scare sullies

the still peace-pond
I have been working on.
How to not feel a failure?

I have worked hard and long,
more than most anyone.
As much is healed,

more is revealed.
Tears profusely flow from
the inevitable layers of the onion.

Whatever I thought
I would be and do...?
How not to feel a failure?

Every day I get up,
I eat, I keep on
with tasks needing to be done.

As to life purpose
as to what work seemed to matter most,
what of that?

How to remember grace and be grateful?
How to be patient and trust...
enough?

12/31/09

A Way to Release Sorrow
After Tricia's call

I am me
but small
falling into
the vat of sorrow.

You are right
it is not endless
and I do not drown
just fall and fall

until I reach bottom,
and I invoke
something innate
to clear it out.

But first I
remember to ask
the source.
A movie begins

but very fast,
not for me to see
each scene or image
just let it play out

to the ending.
And it does end.
The gist of it is
all the medical things

done without regard
to violation,
but no one thing

the cause or solution,

just let the movie play,
holding a sacred space.
Then invoke the emptying
a giant vacuum of a sort

not matter, not visible
except in action.
I am at vat-bottom
holding my arms up in a "V"

and the sorrow is leaving me,
leaving a delicious temporary
spaciousness
which I fill with joy.

At first a heavy gel
which does not seem right.
I stop, clear, and begin again.
What is joy

in manifestation?
Light…bubbles…colors…birds…
songs…dancing…sunsets…flowers.
I feel it as it fills the vat.

I am covered over
yet not drowning,
saturated and flowing
on the day of the blue moon,

last day of the decade,
the end and the beginning.
Be still.
Let it be.
So be it.
Amen.

12/31/09

Small Hope

In the darkness
everything is covered
in that dampening blanket
even a pinhole of light
makes all the difference.

2010

1/8/10

Soave
From Llubav

Speak to yourself in a soft voice
I know this has been a tough time.

Soave.
Be gentle.

1/9/10

Flying Geese

The leader at the "V" point changes
so the responsibility of bearing the brunt,
breaking the flight path, does not fall on any one
even exceptionally strong goose,

but is borne by many if not all the flock in turn.
Watch the sky one day to see how they effortlessly
change position, keeping an even space between,
straightening the crooked line,

without complex speech or obvious negotiation,
without campaign, voting or capitulation.
Each seems to know their place
in the grand scheme

as if
they were all connected,

as if all
were the whole.

1/11/10

Because My Star

Because my star
is tied to yours

my love,
my life is entwined

with your own.
And what you do

or say or think or feel
and what you do not do

or say or think or feel
affects me too.

Some days I wish
it was not so,

that I was not so vulnerable,
that I was like

anyone else, but
then would you have

been drawn to my beacon?
And would I have

recognized when
my heart sang?

1/14/10

Selective Memory

I do not remember
the trouble walking,
though for years
my dearest heart-wish
was to walk without
limp or conscious thought.

I am only aware of
where I am and what is
now going on,
what healing is yet undone.
I forget where I came from...
until I remember.

Each unique healing celebration,
each specific restoration,
each longing answered,
each one revealing
another layer to the onion,
another valley of tears

until the crying was done,
the splinters again as one
in the structure and function,
heart cracked wide open...
and that is a very good thing,
yes-sir-ee.

1/20/10

Something Small
After listening to Poetry Center CD

You can write a poem
about anything:

mundane, mystical, trivial
momentous, silly or banal.

A car in front of me
on a dark winter night,

not even snowing
or particularly cold,

the car about to turn right
when the flasher lights went on,

slowly completing the turn
as I did behind, and

out popped a son,
not mine, but someone's,

and began to push
the cream-colored Ford sedan,

and then, presumably the father
sprang out of the passenger door

wearing a gray knit cap,
an ordinary coat, and also put his muscle to it.

Someone behind me long-tooted
as I edged around,

but what can you do really
when a car that had been

reliable, suddenly wasn't,
or maybe there were warning signs

unattended or maybe gas ran out
or gages were broken,

whatever it was,
a bit of grace please,

a small prayer,
or gold glitter energy sprinkles,

if not more substantive aid.
It could happen to anyone.

Do unto others….
What goes 'round, comes 'round.

1/22/10

Ask and Response

Who among us
has given up,

let slide the imperative,
the drive to create,

to be present?
Who has not given up

in the dark-pit times,
the apparent endlessness

of the drop down,
the fall from grace

it seems like it,
though grace is not

won or lost
it just is

like a money cushion in the bank
always to fall back on,

always replenished.
I only ask the obvious question

not expecting any real answer.
But the echo comes back to me

from the grandest canyon,
the edge of the precipice,

"Yes, of course."

1/23/10

Speaking Kidney

Do you speak kidney,
can you tell what would
comfort or support?

How to encourage and
not neglect or dominate,
if not...consequences.

What would kidney language be like?
Like the earth speaking
in ebb and flow of tides,

crying softly in drought or deluge,
flowing currents coming and going,
pushing and pulling.

We are on average 60% water they say
all under the domain
of the gentle bean kidneys.

Be firm they say,
do not get distorted
by the messy chaos of life

however enticing.
Drink water pure and plentiful,
excrete toxins and excess.

Allow the elegant system
to work without manual control,
only listen...and allow.

1/25/10

Family Photo

She is not in the picture,
but I can feel her there almost in the frame,

standing back from us, my camera in her hand,
small Mona Lisa smile on her lips, frown of concentration.

The four of us lined up dressed in our best
on a sunny fall day in front of a big tree.

And what would later shatter
has not happened yet.

The wind was calm and it did not rain,
unlikely we will ever go there again.

2010, Surgery

2/9/10

Complications

The world has gotten so small:
this bed, this room
and barely down the hall.

No expansive intelligent interior space,
no writing, no educated linear reasoning.
Where am I in all this?

My carefully tended garden,
my humor, my patience, my trust
as what was planned, collapsed.

Dramatic pain
grabs the attention,
brooks no neglect,

from nothing to everything,
all nerves on alert,
no food, no sights, no smells

bear their usual kindness.
To be thrust into the situation,
the place, that felt most...unsafe

(energetically speaking),
to find a way through darkness,
to ask for and accept even unlikely help.

2/11/10

Comfort

Sometimes the need for comfort is so acute,
the circumstances so dire and dark,
the vortex you are pulled into so nightmarish,

everything taken away: food, water, sleep, all the familiar,
that you can't find yourself within yourself,
you are a skin filled with nothing in particular

and it seems you will always be lost.
Even if someone is there who knows you well,
whose voice is the tether to reality,

who casts the line, holds the rod that reels you in,
even then
the need for comfort is so great

that anything from home,
any ice chip or thoughtfulness,
any kindness or generous voice

calls you back to hopefulness.

2/11/10

Consternation

I don't want to remember last week,
analyze the gory details:

what went right,
what went wrong and why.

I don't want to use it in writing,
preserve memory on the page.

Already details slip away
and I am grateful.

What is useful will stick
I am certain,

the rest is being
healed and forgotten.

Blessed oblivion.

The opposite of my usual.

2/17/10

Hold On

There are no words
for what has happened,
telling the literal story
does not help.

Trust uncovered as betrayal—
not true, but feels true.
In the big picture
this is but a dot,

trivial almost
and that also does not help.
For this is a place of
only darkness

where I have landed again,
no obvious entrance or exit.
Even knowing I got out
last time does not illuminate.

Even all previous work
and skill and support
does not help me now.
Time and sky and beauty

may restore some energy,
but here, where I am,
that is hard to hold onto
when I had vowed:

never again.

I see how the drugs
were given for a reason
(no one really reads
the brochures for contraindications),

I see how harsh circumstances
no food, no sleep, extreme pain
could have ripped off the skin
I so carefully cultivated.

If I did once
I can again...
just hold on.

2/24/10

Beginning a Very Long List

I am grateful for fading of images
burned on the pliant leather of my mind.

I am grateful for forgetfulness and forgiveness—
for me included.

Some things I don't want to remember and write about,
teach and ponder. I am the ever-changing center of it all.

I am grateful for the people who came to help me heal:
those in my circle, those who did one small essential thing.

I am grateful for insides that stay in
and strong muscles, intact skin.

I am grateful to be pain-free, to wear regular clothes,
to eat and digest food, to laugh and blow bubbles.

I am grateful for sleep, for reading, to be able to write.
For clear mind, to climb stairs,

to be able to get out of bed by myself.
I am grateful to drive, to go off alone...and safe.

I am grateful for massage and colored light,
acupuncture, guided imagery, talking, and healing energy.

I am grateful for breaths that soak deep into my body, for heart
pumping in steady rhythm, blood flowing freely in vessels.

I am grateful for clean clothes and fresh sheets,
a cozy comfortable nest of a bed,

warm showers and coconut bubbles sluicing over clean skin,

for generous husband, kind children, concerned family.

I am grateful for a future stretching out with possibility.
I am grateful for taste and smell, hearing, touch and sight,

for returning clarity and balance, peace and harmony.
I am grateful for timely Olympics, Elizabeth Peters, and Enya.

I am grateful for my fun blue Mini Cooper in need of cleaning.
For snowy days soon ending in spring, for passing seasons,

crisp air, watercolor clouds, intermittent sun.
I am grateful for warmth and water, softness and firmness,

promise of returning strength, for blue nails like an ocean
in the desert, for girls' day out, replenishing, restoring.

I am grateful for what is coming, for juicy, rich days ahead
and for what is past, healed and done.

No, I do not need to remember all the dark abyss details
to be grateful I made it again to light.

Did I forget the Loving Others, those guiding ever-present
spirits? I didn't mean to.

The list is long and continuing:

a comfort bear brought to the hospital,
a timely shoulder rub and discussion of the history of Jell-O,

story-telling, a sweet kiss, encouraging words,
so much gratitude every cell is filled with it.

2/24/10

Room on Cardiology Floor

I can still feel her surprisingly soft lips
pressing on my forehead,
a good bye and good luck kiss as she left.

My roommate, sweet Italian lady,
both of us not our best, faces pale,
hair tangled and matted.

Her husband, most kind, friendly and hopeful,
full of stories with ambulances and happy endings.
How he'd been recognized

by the ambulance driver in the grocery store.
How she'd had a seizure maybe
and he'd carried her to the door

though he had a pacemaker and they were older.
All her surgeries and still her spunk.
"Good bye," she said, "It will be fine,"

or something like that in her gentle Italian accent,
pressed into my hopeless forehead.
Unexpected, spontaneous, natural and welcome.

Three weeks later I feel the kiss still.
Her easy gesture, her faith,
her sweet kindness.

Of course she was right.

2/24/10

Gratitude

Because I choose,
what I am left with is gratitude.

I am grateful for a calm, confident, good-humored surgeon
and not needing him to be my best friend.

I am grateful for Nicolette and Adona and Cara and Ylang,
and all the nurses and PCs and transport people

at an amazingly friendly hospital with no students to teach,
for sterile supplies and makers of special mesh,

for all the smiling blue-gowned surgical nurses including
"Granny."

For Tricia and Geary and Lisa and Brigitte and Kip
who helped me prepare before and heal after.

2/25/10

How I Choose to Tell the Story

Punch line first,
how it all turns out fine,
how I am not the victim of anything.

Some of the dark details or none
stripped of inevitable drama,
how all help was there for me,

how much I have recovered,
how I am in no pain
in spite of everything.

Leave out the disorientation,
the evoked depression,
the endless feeling of despair,

for from this vantage point
back in steady light,
from this somewhat balanced perception

...again
 I trust all is well.

3/2/10

Post Surgery Follow-Up
After Tricia...again

Would you be willing
 to let go the good for the better,

let down defenses, dissolve armor,
release grievances old and new

to expose the true you,
the power, the creation, the ultimate vision?

Who else could but you?

Allow excision of adhesions and scars,
liquefy the crust of a hard life,

let go misunderstandings, expectations,
false beliefs blocking radiant sun?

Remember before you coalesced
and emerged here from your cocoon

when you could fly like a dream,
when thought and action were one?

That is still who you are...
buried within somewhere

and waiting...
if not now, when?

3/6/10

Deer

Their cloven hooves cut
through fluff and crust of snow.
By their marks we know
just where the deer would go,

how close to house, how far,
what trees they delicately nibble,
what summer-vine or spring flowering bush,
what green they sought

in thick white snow
to keep deer body aligned with deer soul.
Crossing the fields one more day
is all a witness can fairly say.

Their impressive muscular hugeness,
tiny heads, big-flicker ears perked up,
each strand of fur, brown nose, soft eyes,
one foot from me through my kitchen window.

Then...away, white tails high,
into near woods, then deeper, and deeper still
to where these three would stay the night
quiet if not ever sleep deep.

3/7/10

Inspired
Song by Danny Schmidt at Folkstage

To sit in patience
and walk in patience
and swim in patience

trusting.
To not wish for things
to be other than they are

and if sun darkens for a while
to remember
this too shall pass.

3/9/10

Recipe
For Lisa and me

Feather brush
back in balance

feather brush
feather brush

No cannonballs
over the bow

that hit the vitals
and sink the ship

—or almost
whatever stated good intention.

Ignorance is no excuse
nor what was taught,

the truth is the truth
captured if sought.

Not a victim, no,
healing certain even so,

one feather or a few
same for me, same for you.

3/15/10

If I Had Known

would I have chosen?
I suspect not
and yet...
this is one kind of
perfection

3/20/10

Mustering Illusive Understanding

When I read what I had written—
words both sparse and heartfelt—
darkness again descended unbidden.

And all I could do was curl up,
cry, and wait, voiceless.
Already I had worked, healed, and released,

surprised the depths could still ambush me
with their unexpected ferocity.
And all I could do was call out

and religiously breathe to calm,
retreat into useful intuitive distraction,
and wait in relative silence

until whatever time must pass,
whatever sands must blow into the jagged holes,
covering exposed nerves and raw memory.

And whatever I am to become
from all this…
comes.

3/23/10

Close from a Distance
Another for my mother...and me

She looks into the mirror
and sees an old woman there,
though she does not believe she is old,
though she well remembers
her youth and energy.

Allowing her mind to
drift back in time
reviewing life lived deeply
and a body deeply scored
by thirty thousand days passing.

Not an easy life she chose,
it was honest and tough, joyful and messy
and she is close to her natural end.
The lines on her face have deepened,
her well-formed cheeks have sunken,

her eyes and ears dimming, present still but
mind clinging more to wisps of the past
and more words now elude her in frustration.
Often she feels lonely or gets bored.
She is getting ready to pass

but grasps still to a thick branch
on the bank of the river.
I send all love to her from here
and say it is OK to stop struggling
and drift sweetly, easily on,

OK to just let go, peaceful and calm.

4/6/10

Life Skill

Make a list
of pros and cons
recognizing the risk
inherent in any decision
cognizant that not choosing
is still choosing.

And choose.

4/6/10

The Rest of the Story…

And in the end
it might be said
the good outweighed the bad
with mostly good intention,

what wrongs were not righted
were endured, the irritant
around which a pearl could grow
(not all pearls are equally valuable).

Whatever was scarred or lost:
belly, innocence or breast,
would now be crossed off the list—
nothing more to teach,

nothing more to be done or examined.
To make the most of
what is left: what body,
what time, what heart and mind.

To sleep without wishing
things were otherwise, to wake
refreshed, anger and agony acknowledged
but urgently forgotten.

Begin to build from
this vast solid common ground,
the rest of the story yet to be written….

4/10/10

Attitude

Without attention
scars tighten

what was flat
mounds up as

form no longer
follows function

what was elegant design
now seems ugly or

the best of a bad situation
and thus beautiful perfection

6/3/10

Dear Body

It is not right
for fluid otherwise known as serum
to accumulate in a pocket under the skin
to the left of the belly button.
I have tried to do what I can.
Please remove.
Thank you.

Sincerely
Yours Truly

2010, Life Resumes

6/4/10

Aftertaste

Do you know
how it is

when you drink
a fine wine or beer

or eat a luxurious meal
and something lingers

in the mouth after,
some taste definable or

unnamable, pleasurable or no,
exotic or ordinary

to be savored or
washed away?

That's how I want to be:
refreshing with a hint of mystery

surprisingly sweet
with a generous dollop of honesty.

6/8/10

Reconsider

If
to be with you

is
to be numb to

part of me
that retreats to

shadow,
I may decide

not to.

6/8/10

Ultimately Hopeful Witness

It is not just procrastination,
crude theft of future time,

it was the remodeling,
the juggling too many balls,

the surgery, the emergency,
the adult children

returning home (like their peers)
taking up time and space

in some quantum fashion.
It was life unfolding,

and parents aging,
and body aching and sleep lacking

that led to the undesired
pressured outcome.

But wait! Surely
the rest can still be re-written.

6/9/10

Left Wanting

I thought
if I could walk
smooth like anyone

life would be
well, better
even all better.

But it has become
another thing
taken for granted

on the way to wanting
the next thing.

6/12/10

Shadow Healing
James Keelaghan at Folkstage

What part of me
is overflowing

What part is a
river dammed up

What part of me
longs for release

What part is tears
flowing unbidden

What part is unkind
or uncertain

I'm only saying
trying to decode a language
spoken in symptoms

trying to heal what
has arisen.

What part of me
is unbending

What part needs
immediate release

What is becalmed
stilled, expressionless

What is inflamed or angry
deserving to be heard

What is in shadow
unforgiven, denied

What part is unloved
buried deep, pushed aside

What is impatient, impotent
small, voiceless

worthy of healing
worthy of being part

of the perfect again-
welcome whole.

What part of me is
weakness unacknowledged

What part is unwilling to rest
and restlessness

What part of me is
tears un-shed and
fears hidden and
words bitten back

What have I walled off
what am I pregnant with

What desperate pleas
have gone unanswered

What part of me is
warring against another

What is revealed
comes up for air

what comes up
light shines upon it

what has light
has hope and promise

anything is possible
anything is possible to heal.

Don't give up
anything is possible.

6/18/10

Escape Velocity
Offspring

To leave again the velvet nest,
warm, feathered comfortable,
food provided and support,

where love is foundation
and you know someone has your back,
the cold realities of daily life blunted.

It takes some doing
I can tell you
to pack up and head out,

join the trek.
That's where life is,
the hard knocks, the jostles

the insights, the Hallelujahs,
where the people are,
the relationships that test and teach

and years pass in complicated fullness.
Yes, all true.
But to leave the home, the nest

knowing how it is...
pulled nevertheless...
to choose freedom.

7/17/10

Convert the Pain

to fuel

the fallen blossoms
recycle

what *was* into
what can be

if only.

Nothing is
certain and

anything is
possible.

You thought it was
a child's fable

but it's true
as true as anything.

7/17/10

Not Exactly Recrimination

I wish I could tell you
I learned every lesson hard-won
and remembered later
and made the changes

even in tiny baby steps.
That I used my stubbornness
on my own behalf, but
I have to report

I am like anyone who struggles
who juggles, who is faced with troubles
and forgets to ask for help
forgets to rest.

Forgets all the past grace
and falls off the cliff
until attention is paid
and recollection.

Oh, if self-love were easy,
everyone would do it!

7/18/10

Sitting With It

My Uncle Tom died last week,
my Dad's only brother,

I was not that close to him
so the intensity of my grieving

ambushed me.
But he represented my father,

gone these 25 years,
and he represented my past, my childhood,

my tribe, my clan (all that expectation).
All the memories wrapped up in one man.

He represented all the aunts and uncles beginning to pass on
and my mother, waiting in line.

I am from Michigan people who gathered
and stayed together, supported each other.

I left them to find myself—
the gain in that decision

greater than the loss, but there was loss nevertheless,
any connection to them from a distance.

Any relationship of my children to them,
more fragile and tenuous.

(My children did not grow up like me with
extended family at every important occasion.)

Now my Dad's only brother is gone...
no more chances for understanding.

7/19/10

To Err on the Side of Caution

is still erring
with good intention,

a mother's tightrope
over a gaping chasm,

balance only momentary
help often illusory.

How to know how much advice—
and when—is right and necessary?

When to step back
when to hang on

how much to risk
how big the possible mistake

how hard to watch
how old the child

how to avoid the pitfall
"if only I had"...?

7/26/10

Real Cactus

Reflex
to bare-handed
catch

a cactus
grown too tall
for buried roots

grown since
a 6-inch baby
now 4 feet

and falling
dirt flying.
Who wouldn't

at least try
to save.
Who would

think then
of sharp spines
broken in finger skin.

8/3/10

Yes, I Noticed You Being You

What can I say of friend Amy
who spoke tonight so well and courageously,

who opened arms wide, glad to see me
before I even stepped through the door.

Who generously watches out for me
and graciously accepts me.

How fine a friend is that!

Amy, who paints her sad tale so vividly
parts of it are funny,

disconcerting when she feels more the tragedy,
but she pulls us into the humanness of the story

and humor allows us to keep looking,
to keep listening to what was imaginably unbearable.

A skilled weaver, illusionist, wordsmith,
she makes me care...what happens next.

8/4/10

Doors (3)
IWWG at Brown

Back doors, front doors, side doors,
creaky doors, easy-slide patio doors,
temperamental doors depending on the weather.

From inside looking out
from out, looking in
perspective is everything.

Certain door types found in certain areas of town,
but the most worn so far, with the substantial hole
in the bare wood splintered step

is one short block from the college dorm
and the chichi, multicolor-trimmed,
ornate pillared-porch door.

Doors with transoms, doors with fanlights,
double doors, single doors, slim or wide,
doors with chains, doors with brass handle locks,

doors with deadbolts, doors with beveled windows,
doors with gates, doors with peepholes,
gates with latches, wrought iron elaborate

or parallel bare bars like a fence,
multi-panel doors, or flat veneer or select fine wood,
revolving doors, automatic doors, doors to push or pull.

Doors that stay open, doors that swing shut
doors that slam every time, screen doors,
doors with jalousie window slats and aluminum frames.

Bathroom doors, kitchen doors, bedroom doors,
Dutch doors where the top separates from the bottom.
In fifty-eight years, how many doors have I walked through:

school doors, library doors, store doors, church doors,
restaurant doors, house doors, rest stop doors, apartment
doors, car doors, public doors, private doors,

doors to keep out or let in,
revealing or concealing everything.

8/8/10

Thinking of You

Time and again
I faced an inevitable end

and thus far
it always receded

to the indefinite future
where you still are.

8/8/10

Lie Down

Lie down in the clouds above you

separate for a moment from the life you lead

float for a bit weightless

just for a moment

then drift back

light

breathe

and re-animate

wiggle bare toes, feel grass tickle

feet grounded but light on the face of earth

8/9/10

Someone Said

Someone said something
a small puzzle
a sliver under the skin

irritatingly hard to remove.
Why of all the kind words spoken
should these thoughtless ones remain?

Because of implication
because I want to please everyone
(including me)

even though that is not possible—
there is no pleasing some people.
Let it go, don't you know.

Let it go, my sweet potato.
Talk and untangle.
Walk and calm.

Sweat and sleep and write
and bless all the teachers
who have come.

Bless and move along.

8/16/10

Saturday Morning

She woke alone to fresh blood
streaming between her legs
and when she abruptly stood,
clots on the new tan carpet.

Though not in pain
and not the first time, she was 58,
ovaries in protective custody
and finished with all that.

How much she had done
over and over again
to avoid
just such a thing.

Though not in pain
it was shocking
and of course...
inherent betrayal.

8/23/10

Suggestible from a Distance

He emailed her a
graphic picture,
close-up of tangled legs,

large mattress-squashed striped bug
wanting a name,
put in a category

of worrisome things.
It was nighttime
and she was to a degree, bug-phobic,

suggestible, but knowledgeable
from years of curiosity
and wide observation.

Possibility: centipede?
Google search:
exact photographic match.

Now *she* felt like the one
who had been unpleasantly surprised
though neither was in fact bitten.

She felt wary and alert
to each trickle of sweat,
each brush of her sheets,

each breath of wind
on exposed night skin.
No matter how many times

the image was put out
it crept back in.
He is her son. She would do it again.

8/30/10

Memorial to a Joyful Life

I want to write about Charlie,
what I remember most vividly:
How at Christmas in the 1980's he complimented

my burgundy, cigarette high heels,
the ones I wore with the cowl-neck
pale gray sweater dress, so soft to the touch.

How he danced with such exuberant
vibrant vitality at Chris and Llubav's wedding
he could have been any age.

That one Thanksgiving he and Dorothy rented a limo
for the nieces and nephews and spouses
for the surprise in downtown Detroit.

How he was fit and kind, solicitous and generous,
always in company with his beloved, Dorothy.
How his eyes had that crinkle-sparkle

as if life held anything but disappointment.
Yet he was in the army, four years in the big war,
and must have seen things, had dreams that didn't come true.

He lived to eighty-six
joyful right up to the quick end—
a deep brain tumor...and he was gone.

Now she is on her own
in that surreal space between
what was then...

and what will become
the new normal.
I do not worry for her,

she is spunky and strong.
She has an extensive close network of friends
built from two lives in motion.

She is aware and gracefully holding on.
There will be bad days of pain
and many days she still talks to him.

But her life stretches out ahead,
much to do, worthy causes to gratefully serve
before she can close her eyes...

and finally rest.

9/10/10

The Mechanics of Healing

To imagine a version of myself
without illness,
without a trace of bitterness
at what was done or undone.

To remember I am never alone
without resources or kindness,
to be balanced, strong and calm,
living clean in the day to day

uninfluenced by subconscious
misinterpretations, misunderstandings,
false assumptions passed down,
unhealed breaches of trust and confidence.

To not find fault with myself,
not judge harshly as my default position,
to reset expectation back to the beginning
when life stretched out pure and promising.

9/11/10

What I Saw

Luminous sliver-moon,
bright star or planet, maybe Venus
off to the lower right.

Day-globe has gone, clear and then
smear of orange on the horizon,
black-green trees in lacy silhouette.

Polished marble headstones
tilt at the exact correct angle
to glimmer-shine in fading light.

A jet flies silently unnoticed
between moon and trees
in evident safety.

All is still and beautiful.
Darkness falls and
all is still and beautiful.

9/13/10

Affirming

To welcome the mesh
reinforcing the hole
keeping the insides in.

To allow merging and melding
of mesh and muscle
full diaphragmatic breathing,
belly expands, contracts, expands....

To love, to be grateful
for all parts comprising
the healing whole
for all the efforts

expended and contemplated
to be continued....

9/15/10

For Lisa and Me

I can't tell you the answers,
you are you and I am me
and though we have similarities
we are each unique
in the totality of human history.

I can tell you a story
both true and imaginary, and you
might borrow a word or reference or two
as a missing piece in your own complexity.

You might weave one of my threads
into the new tapestry you are creating
and if it seems just right
you would keep it with my blessing.
Always it is you doing the choosing.

If you want it to work
but it does not, I would hope
you'd keep on searching.
For you will recognize in whatever guise
what is you and what is not
even if you temporarily forget.

You are beauty incarnate.
You are radiant love.
You are light playing on the river at sunrise.
And even in occasional despair,

try to remember.

9/20/10

Not Exactly a Memoir

Chapter one
she is born

or first the prologue
what can't be undone.

She is a daughter
a sister. She laughs, she crawls,

she walks, eats, sleeps, drools,
all the usual.

She grows until
time for school.

She is shaped
by what did and did not

happen, where she lived and when,
who was born after or before.

Chapter two
public then Catholic schools,

trying to fit in
and not succeeding,

trying to be smaller
even invisible,

learning to please, to anticipate,
making mistakes, the salvation of reading.

Chapter three
gets better you'll see.

Further shaping, smoothing the rough stone
in the tumbler of life away from home.

Tumultuous times, rules redefined,
doors open that had been closed,

a chance meeting leads to
a lifetime tryst.

More growing, flesh covers
the raw barnacles.

Chapter four
there's more.

Husband, more school, children, house, jobs,
diagnoses smack upside the head,

abrupt changes in direction
devastation and reflection.

Chapter five
she comes alive.

From the bog she rises
Phoenix-like, reborn, transformed.

She begins again
and again....

Stay tuned,
more to come.

10/7/10

Dodge Poetry Festival #5

Can I make a happy home
in this magnificently scarred body?
so at odds with where I thought I'd be,

beyond repair, but not beyond redemption.
Look what I am attracting in...
healing, beauty, satisfaction...
reason for hope...then.

10/8/10

When You Left a Hole to Fill
October, Newark, #8

How boring it would be
if we both loved poetry,
brought the same plates
of plain or fine food to the table
we still gratefully share.

Instead, you are the mirror image of me
though not in any particular,
you are the artist with food
as I am with words,
you are the a-scientific J.D.
and I have the Ph.D. in microbiology,

you are the more coordinated, athletic one,
and we share a taste for photography.
How is it then we came together
thirty-eight years and counting?
How is it we have ridden out
every terrible storm,

resolved each inevitable conflict?
Not always mutual agreement—
that would be impossible—
not through denial, sweeping thorns under the rug,
I am too tenacious and you, the trial lawyer,
can be too pugnacious for that.

It is mystery and shared commitment,
stubbornness and sheer blind luck
that when tsunami waves crashed over us
we clung to each other,
and when crisis after crisis ended,
perspective was restored and love renewed.

And we were able to remember
how very much we like being together.

10/9/10

Dodge Poetry Festival #11

What is it you most fear
that you will succeed or fail
that you will die unknowing

Or do you fear love or
being unloved even by
your own self for yourself

Whatever it is, surface or buried
whatever the details
smack fear in the face directly

and walk away.

10/11/10

Book Signing: Kay Ryan

I said how natural she was on stage.
She said poets are just people you know—
it felt like wry chastisement—
not knowing I am a poet
and I was learning by watching her,
absorbing, not just listening and laughing.

Often poets who read are not
willing to risk being themselves
in all delicious quirkiness
in all complex humanness
in front of everyone
wanting rather, to be perfection
or some reasonable approximation.

10/11/10

Just Before Tops Diner

I am not ready to leave the river
with its infinite variations
and endless fascinations

its effortless sliding over the earth
playing with wind and sun
the birds, the fish, the nightlights

the river as mirror
with ever-changing reflections.
But the river I suspect

is unmoved by my moving.
What change have I wrought
by my wistful longing

and incessant watching?
What can I take of it
back with me into life?

How the river never gives up
even if it seems to be going backward.
How something new can always happen.

Today after 5 days of observation
the first boat cuts across the mirror surface
making delicious patterns of thick wake.

I will miss this river
its width, its depth
its breadth, its calm

the unexpected gift of its presence
flowing along, flowing along.
But if I don't leave, I miss…

this.

10/14/10

Reaction
For Lynn S.

It began with rhyme
and you thought you knew
where this was headed

the regularity of it
the rhythm a comfort.
Then the rhyme

disappeared, leaving you dangling
wanting the familiar
wishing for the expected.

That was the point
or part of it—that life is like that
sometimes, a rug pulled from under—

and poetry only reflection
...or reaction.

10/15/10

The Day After the Call
For John

For some while
he has been dying
a day at a time

more overtly than
the rest of us
dying year by year.

Now he is
in the place of grace
dying hour by hour.

What to do
to help him now
with whatever his purpose.

What to do
to help us now
learn from this

to be kinder
gentler
more generous.

Time here is short
in the big scheme of things...
and elsewhere is long...

remember this.

10/18/10

Prayer for My Youngest Brother

They said nothing more could be done,
get your affairs in order, this week could be the end…
and that was true in their realm,

in their experience, a kindness.
Nevertheless, there is more than this:
Miracles happen, unexplained and unexplainable.

What I would wish for you is simple:
Before you go, do what you came to do,
that when the door closes you are satisfied.

Until then I ask all help to come to you
in whatever form, to do what can be done in my realm,
what blessing, what elucidation, what healing

to ease struggle in the body, erase the pain
bring peace and harmony to your mind,
calm emotions, support the spirit—each connected to all—

to encourage hopefulness, eliminate helplessness,
gentle rain of grace upon you, as ever an unearned gift to us.
Until the last breath I ask for this. Amen.

10/19/10

At Odds

If you
had known
what you
know now
would you
do it
better

or would
you make
the same
mistakes
over
and over?

Could you
try this
one thing
once and
see what
happens:

Self-love,
even
simple
kindness?

10/20/10

For Robert Pattinson
And the others

To be the perfect mirror
so that others see
what they most desire

is a special kind of hell.
To not be real,
anything your own,

celebrated but
not seen.
Invisible in your own skin,

when you step out
the image you created
precedes and masks you.

Who takes the trouble
to get to know you
in all quirky human complexity?

The more you say
"I am not a fictional character,"
the less you are believed,

an immense price to pay
for unexpected popularity,
ultimately unsought,

no matter the salary.

11/9/10

What Is Important

Some poems are written
to be mostly filled in

by later listener
who can read into

what was left unsaid
who can see all the

unarticulated possibility
space left for co-creativity

and marvel and judge
as worthy.

11/15/10

Right in Front of Me

How familiar this hand
its form and function
gradually wrinkling skin
now visible veins, tendons

shape of the nails, their strength
history of vigorous, oblivious use.
To remember when young
how much taken for granted. And now,

more towards the end than the beginning
still able to flex, to bend
make a fist, brush a cheek,
to hold a pen, mind open.

11/17/10

Emotional Control

as if that were always a good thing
to not dissolve into a puddle
in front of everyone—or even alone

as if to be exposed to the core
to be that revealing
was somehow unacceptable

would set in motion
a collapse of civilization
instead of the nascent foundation

to be built upon.
There is something to be said
for calm

      true calm
not a lid put on
a boiling volcano

as if no one will sense
the evident falseness
as if trust were just an oft-broken promise.

Emotional control
as if that were always a good thing
to avoid exposure of what

might prove embarrassing
to be honest for once
about how you are feeling

or why or who you are
as a result of the fates or mistakes
or what happened in the course of living.

Emotional control
as if that were always a good thing
a coveted sparkling ring

to be grasped and worn
at all human costs
even permanent numbness

even eventual blindness
the gut and heart put to bed
with all the rest.

11/23/10

Reading *The Cruelest Month* by Louise Penny
With reference to Leonard Cohen and Diana Jones

Is there anyone aware who
does not feel a fraud
as if secrets can no longer be hid,

as if the dark outweighs
any achievement—if only
"they" could see past the veil,

the illusion, the image, the lie perpetuated?
Is there anyone who was and remains
so pure and accomplished, so honest,

who never tried to pass
shine for rust,
who in some corner of some cage,

feared discovery, feared...
feared...feared...until blind and deaf to beauty,
until consumed with self-loathing replacing self-discovery?

Can simple love heal the breach;
and the imperfection—the crack that lets the light in—
lets the light in? Forever. Amen.

11/24/10

For Alex
In Times of Trouble

This may be a relationship
you learn from
or you overcome

or climb a mountain
you thought was impossible
or stretched you thin and then some.

This may be time you learned to support
or to let go of someone or
some preconceived notion,

when you learned to take one step at a time
when you put aside assumptions
and fully lived in the moment.

When you accepted as much love
as you gave, more than you felt
you deserved somehow.

That you looked underneath
and deep and could be kind
and self-loving no matter what.

You healed and became more whole
exactly when you felt your heart was breaking
and stayed with that feeling

to see what it really means,
where it really leads you.
What choices you make in staying true

to your highest vision of yourself,
what gifts come out of darkness.
No matter what, anything living

cannot stay the same, relationships included,
to grasp onto what was good
may block what could be even better.

No one knows the future—
how much time, when, why, or where—
part is given, part created by you.

What courage to do this hard work...
what courage to watch you.

12/21/10

Inevitable Woman Nature?

When I am eighty—
should I make it that far—
I will look back at photos of me now
and see how beautiful
how smooth the skin, bright the eyes
wide the smile, white the teeth
remembering how easy it was to get around
how gracious I was, how lovely my full hair.
Even on the good days at eighty
the me now will favorably compare.
Just like now looking back in time
to when I could only see my younger flaws
and now can see her beauty and grace
and wish I had...
noticed.

12/31/10

The Leaving of It

Part of life
the leaving of it
with what grace and
awkwardness

items still on the list
unfinished business
opportunities now lost
stories, secrets, dreams

what was true once
unknown at best
the mystery unraveled
the tapestry complete.

2011

1/2/11

Waiting in Michigan
Gathering of the clan

There is no doubt about the outcome
not a matter of whether, but when.

A man lays downed
in a hospital gown, barely breathing,

brain shut down, now
a short matter of time till the physical end.

Unresponsive, but cared for
his imminent demise called from coast to coast,

the loving family gathers tearful,
fearful today is the final day.

Saying goodbye
in each unique way,

the stories told
back to childhood,

no more from his memories,
his lips, but

now flowing freely, one prompting another.
Sorrow mixed with laughter.

In some ways known better
than ever in life.

Flaws not forgotten,
put into some perspective

as the tapestry of his life is woven complete.

1/2/11

For Stephen

He tried to control everything
please everyone, make it all right.

Conscious or unconscious that one thing
could not be undone, his father was dying.

Not in that vague someday soon sense,
but a life measured in hours.

Nothing could undo the choices
that led to this,

nothing could give more chances
to redo the old story,

nothing could soothe the pain
that begins a second after waking,

but time,
though right now

the black is breathless-bottomless,
skin flayed, emotions raw on the surface.

His defenses thick from
years of trial law practice

vanished in one instant
after that first unexpected phone call.

1/5/11

Side by Side

Two plain gold bands
from two generations of men
one the father, one the son
both now gone.

One band larger, not quite round:
the father, a rough-about immigrant.
One band smaller, a bit shinier:
the son, thin and fine-boned.

What they thought of each other
what they spoke of, one in Polish,
one in unaccented language of the adopted land,
the bands do not say.

They speak only of commitment
to one woman each,
of working long hours to support a family,
of asking for little that was fancy.

Two plain gold bands
thin, not decorated or heavy,
scuffed with the living of life,
not all that is left.

1/12/11

Healing Grief

I don't want to
account to someone for every minute
even myself

sometimes I need to
just drift

You may be lonely
you may be worried about me
or about life but

I cannot come
sometimes

Sometimes I need
to just float on the river

unknowing, fearlessly
let the flowing gentle water

soothe and comfort me
sometimes

let the soothing water
cleanse and open...sometimes

let the cleansing water
heal and release and console

1/15/11

After

After the initial numbness wears off
there is a certain unreality.
I can still clearly picture him
standing at the top of the narrow driveway
or in the front picture window,
arm raised as we pull out.
Toot, toot. Wave goodbye.

1/16/11

Poetry Reader:
The Times We Are In

The plain, pale young man, regular-featured,
did not take off his ordinary blue-gray cap
or remove his unremarkable gray-tan coat
before he stepped to the microphone and spoke.
Something in his air, how he kept his eyes down,
uneasily shuffling his feet and
how he kept repeating his need to fight evil
and something else indefinable
made you wonder if he had a gun in his satchel
and you being closest or almost
began to consider how to disarm him.

1/18/11

Traveling

At some point
you will drive off or
go through the door
or close your eyes
or drop in your tracks

and that will be that
not that I am dwelling on it
but just now I am aware
of the nature of things
and how you are not here

1/28/11

From the 31st Floor at the Hyatt
Chicago

What you spend your time on
shapes who you become,

choices made on the run
or with full deliberation,

unintended consequences
part of the decisions...

for what is known now
may turn out to be untrue

and what is unknown
may ultimately lead you

by the nose or seat of your pants,
kicking and screaming

or acquiescent, complacent even,
caught in the naked act of

becoming.

2/1/11

For Rae

For a while
you may think
you hear his voice
or expect him to
come in from the other room
just like always,

but he's gone
and you are not crazy,
only grieving,
adjusting and discovering
life such as it is,
as one.

2/12/11

Hanging On
Mom

Slowly she is losing words.
At first familiar medical terms
from her nursing career were
harder to access

then disappeared, now
even common words like "month,"
and forgetting sometimes
what you just said,

but in many ways
still enough to carry on
a reasonable conversation.
For how long?

She knows what is happening
and is frustrated and confused
but with inspiring courage
stops after a few tears

and keeps on...
another day...
another day....

2/17/11

Mom

At some point
often a phone call in the night
and someone you love
is gone. Right now

all I'm saying
is the beginning of the end.
And if I cling to the notion,
the belief, that life is eternal,

still I am aware
it ends in this form
and there will be...soon...
one last hug, one last conversation.

As much as I try
not to think about it,
to be in the moment
where you still are,

still I cry softly
when I consider
you not being here.

2/26/11

In Recovery

Half-black, half-white
balls of fluff
that serve as winter birds

sit atop brittle stalks
of purple coneflowers
gone to seed

and pluck out
what once had been
the eye of the bloom.

As at ease
eating those seeds
from what appeared to be

a precarious perch
or desperate enough
in need of food
to try anything once.

I did overdo
the day I mentioned to you,
not content to feel better

and patiently wait, still
to look out my window
watching the birds.

3/2/11

Mom Back in Hospital

There is a certain inevitability
about the last breath
following loss of hearing, eyesight
slow disintegration of memory, speech
regular rhythm-spark of heart
personality, muscles, joints
especially aching inflexible knees.

And there is relief at the end
of long suffering, and grief
at the loss of all that was
or could have been, and
the last inevitable hug
last lucid conversation.

We are at the apparent abyss
the catalyst, the chrysalis
the caterpillar beginning
disintegration into pupa
reconfiguring into butterfly
unexpected from linear extrapolation

but entirely normal
as the way things are.
Goodbye sweetie,
it's alright to go you know,
it's alright to go.

3/8/11

Mom Report

When I heard she was in pain
worse and worsening
when I heard she told a doctor
he was full of shit

and he wanted to give her again
the bad drug that required
getting stuck twice a week
to test the blood

and she came home from the hospital
again today but did not remember which day
and she was black and blue all over
and her sight was failing more so

and her hearing, and she said
she did not want all this
and she struggled to remain her own person.
Added to the mounting issues:

heart irregularity, unstable blood pressure
massive abdominal hernia,
arthritic joints, fibromyalgia, pain of all sorts
kidneys failing to clear water,
memory and clarity less and lessening.

What could I say
but yes to comfort
yes to a change in focus
from quantity to quality of days

such as remain to her?

3/16/11

Rae's Last Day

I can picture her standing there
in front of the living room picture window
small, fragile, vulnerable, frail

wearing her tan jacket
and matching tan pants
her hair done just so

and I gave her a hug and said
we'd soon see her again
knowing it was nearing the end.

Today was the end
of that complex book,
the last page of dialog written

in a grace-filled hospital room
with loved ones gathered around.
All she needed to slip away

more or less easily, graciously, consciously.
To say and hear "I love you," to laugh,
to be herself. To wrap up long life

to breathe the last sacred breath...
and go.

3/24/11

Early Days

Feeling raw
as if there is no skin,
as if there
will never be skin again,

which isn't true
but feels true
as much as feeling
is allowed.

In the light of day
it may seem normal,
smiles and usual surrounds,
but at night

it is not a nightmare
but the blackest real.
Where are the angels
to surround with rose-cream wings

to protect and keep intact as much as can be?
Where are they
if they haven't yet been asked
and are waiting somewhere in the wings?

What kind of movie is this?
It is not about belief
or how you were raised or taught
or how you reacted against that.

It is a practical matter
of protection, to prevent infection
from seeping in, to rebuild
a selectively permeable strong foundation.

I can say,
but you must do
whatever seems
right to you.

This is the darkest
or close...and it will not
always be thus.
Find out how strong you are...

get some help
waiting to be asked.
They are lined up
right behind you.

I would say
how well you are doing,
how much support
you have given and received.

I would tell you
how this changes everything
and that is not a bad thing
to be open to what life will bring...
to clearly see everything.

You have choices now
about where you will travel and when.
Hold out your hand
and take mine.

Let us see
what we will see.
Let us sing loudly in the streets
free from all convention.

3/30/11

Before/After Dr. Lisa

Wind knocked out
piling on
you check in...

not breathing.
But living
so must breathe

open something
some space
some possibility

walk it off
expand
in rhythm

without paying attention
notice
breathing resume.

Whiplash
waves knock flat
what was standing.

Sucker punched
side-swiped
sticks and stones

may break my bones
earthquakes
mudslides

forest fires
natural and unnatural
disasters of all types.

Get up
one foot, then the other foot
walk as if...

you were headed
somewhere.

4/14/11

Remember Japan
Post-earthquake

Now is the time to help
those who have been forgotten
whose earth swallowed
their homes and
whose sea washed their bodies away.

Who are now off the front page
out of public consciousness
reduced to silence except for
radiation upgrades and occasional aftershocks
and back page human interest.

Yet starving in masses, scanning rubble
that had been neighborhoods for anything familiar.
Painful to imagine.
But the stories, if any, buried where
few might read and be moved to action.

Now is the time to help
put out a hand, a prayer, a dollar, a kindness.
Anything....
Everything matters
to those who have nothing.

5/5/11

Basking in Solitude

To be alone
to be able to take up all the space
breathe all the air in a room

flow from one moment to the next
and next without outside consideration.
Not that I am unhappy with you here,

my dears, but I change
from what could be. I change
to fit your shape, your—

even unspoken—expectation.
Your wanting to be with me
alters time and space.

And that said...
to be alone
more than enough to replenish

can be lonely
and I need you here
to remember me as loving

to bring me back
when I wander off lost.
Never forget...to bring me back,

my love.

5/21/11

Deep Grieving
For Louise

Tell me about your brother,
the beloved who has gone,

how you grew up together,
were close or drifted apart

or both or neither,
but you miss him more than

you thought you could…
and still go on missing.

How the time is coming
to come to grips with parting,

to release something finite
into the infinite.

How to remember
and still let go,

how to love
and still continue…

living.

He is not lost
and through him you have found

the depth, the breadth,
the bittersweet fierceness…

of Love.

5/25/11

Casual Witness

Just as a cardinal
flew west from a branch
of the dripping white pine
a white-tailed deer galloped
east behind the blue spruce

and someone was watching.

6/26/11

Stretching Scars

I work very hard
to stretch and soften the scars
from radiation and multiple surgeries
especially the next to last.

Invisible those scars
under the clothed surface,
and the work it takes to keep going
to make it day to day

invisible also.
I am proud of this healing body
however far from cultural ideal
it has always been.

7/1/11

Good Week: For Amy

You are traveling incognito,
hiding behind dark clouds
where you think I cannot see you.

But like the full moon on a fall night
your light radiates unknowingly
through the cracks, around the edges

and the moonbeams are unmistakable.
When the clouds clear, as they always do,
there is the face of the moon.

Raucous, naturally reflective, funny, brilliant
not by effort,
it is just the moon being the moon.

7/30/11

Watching Boats on the Lake
Navy Pier, Chicago

With lips unused to kissing
kisses sought and won
and won again
better this time.

Remembering kissing
as part of everyday living
coming, going, being together
reluctantly pulled apart.

Memorable kisses that drew breath
from your lungs to mine, that lasted forever
or almost, but not quite
kisses that bandaged or bonded

not like super glue, but like braided silk
threads, deceptively strong together
though apparently fragile, soft and thin.
Nothing could prematurely part them.

Lips longing to be asked
afraid of disappointment
or afraid of nothing after all this
still open with promise.

In the course of things, both before and after
speed boats, sailboats, police boats, cruise ships,
fireboats, skiffs, sloops, dinghies, jet skis, tugboats, pirate boats
and one four-masted, gaff-rigged schooner.

Sun sets in the west as expected
behind the striking city skyline silhouette.
Left over sun plays on ripples

as the golden slant slowly turns dark.

Mosquitoes buzz
gulls swoop
air is still and clear,
we could see the smoke stacks

all the way to Calumet Harbor.
Nowhere to go, but here
a witness to life unfolding
no rush. To remember life could be like this.

8/15/11

For My Mother
Who is still here

If I think about
where this is all going
I'll cry again

but if I am here
as I said I would be
we talk and we listen

in easy gentle conversation.
If I don't jump ahead
or fall behind

then, right here
in the middle of
nowhere in particular

I am content.

8/19/11

Ten Days Left—Give or Take
Leaving for grad. school

This is a unique
and valuable time
never to be repeated
when you are your age
and experience
and I am mine.

When what we have to offer
each other is obvious
on the mirror surface
like a perfectly ripe juicy peach
plucked from a well-nurtured tree

we planted long ago.
Though you must go
to continue to grow
I wanted you to know
I love you so.

8/23/11

Grieving as Part of Life
For Evan

Each person who leaves
leaves a hole until
what is left
is the lace of your life,

holes of variable
sizes, shapes, depths
that resonate but do not merge,
each revealing a bit more

of the pattern, the weft
and heft of days,
if not the purpose,
the grand scheme.

What is left is more than
what was removed though
it doesn't feel that way at first.
At first numbness then

awareness only of what is empty,
missing, lost. The mind constantly
strays there like a tongue to a jagged tooth.
Slowly intentional consciousness

returns heightened, senses sharpened,
suddenly becoming a beagle who sniffs
a hundredfold more smells,
an artist painfully naked and exposed.

Gradually new skin grows
over the raw wound
which may continue to heal forever,

not every moment, like now,

but now and then.

8/30/11

Strength

Strong enough to be
weak sometimes

to melt into a puddle
to lose everything familiar

to trust you will be caught
or if not, that

falling is not the end of the world
as you know it.

Strong enough to cry
in front of someone, even a stranger

not just genteel tracks of tears
quietly streaming down wet cheeks

but racking heartbroken sobs
that shudder and shoulder-shake.

Strong enough to feel...
anything...everything

and not get washed away...
to stand your ground.

Strong enough...and enough...
to be flexible in the storm

to bend and not break
to dig back out of the black pit

to pick back up off the ground
though ragged and bruised

to rise up again...and live.

9/12/11

An Ordinary Conversation

My mother wanted to remember
and I want to remember

this particular conversation
which started out about disarray

of a problematic week and
took a journey to calm consideration

of life as it plays out.
And if her voice is rough, throat dry

and if memory slips in and out
well, so what? Here we are still

talking of past and mostly present
telling stories that mean something

lending support, encouragement
eye to eye, heart to heart.

What could be better than that?

9/22/11

Road Kill

Fresh dead squirrel
road kill
as if the road did the deed
as if no human intervention
squirrel not paying attention

9/26/11

Sniping

At first teasing
a bit of a jab
nothing serious, not to wound
really.
And the counter-punch
the escalation,
retaliation
becomes the habit.
Unaware of consequence,
the steady erosion
of stock-piled goodwill,
the descent inherent in disharmony.
Until one day
the two part in acrimony
or the other obvious if rarely chosen
choice
to become conscious, aware
to feel, remember the love
that brought them together
to forgive and
stop the shooting.

9/27/11

True Yoga
In blessing to my teachers

It is not about competing with
anyone else, even my former self,
for flexibility, strength, grace.

It is not about concern
over whether I should risk a pose,
choose the harder variation, or stay in longer.

It is not about the workout, the perceived goal,
though that might be the result.

It is not about blindly following an instruction,
inner listening and I will know.

It is not about no pain, no gain,
push a bit harder.

It is about giving
true, honest, calm consideration.

It is about being present
and breathing, being kind.

It is about incorporation and rest,
honoring and gratitude.

It is about listening to the body speaking.

It is about courage and willingness.

It is not mere tolerance,
but actual acceptance.

10/18/11

Hard Fall

The fall
not from grace
but from briskness,
momentum following
ordinary laws of physics.

One moment laughing,
walking, talking,
the next stumbling,
falling, sprawling
into the street

between the curb and
a new brown parked sedan.
From a good day (finally!)
to unbearable pain
embarrassment, shame.

Try to rise
try to dust off
try to see
to act normally
pretending...

but not possible.
Halsted Street and buildings
melt into bright light,
few outlines remain
and the pain

takes over everything.
Not a head hit,
not bleeding,
scraped knees swelling

from inside pants

(material still intact!).
Left shoulder
hit cement curb and though
mind and will are strong as ever,

eyes close.
She retreats into the bubble
forming around her,
hard to stay with him
despite intense entreaties.

Ambulance gurney,
lying down she returns,
shock retreats.
Emergency room.
X-rays. Testing.

Telling the same story
of what happened 20 times.
More herself, joking even.
Flashbacks
play inside her eyelids,

over and over she stumbles
and falls...and falls,
trying to rise on bruised knees.
Nothing broken,
healing begun immediately,

she remembered to take *Arnica*
tablets to minimize bruising.
Also the best of it:
her left side hurt, not dominant right,
no blood or ragged gash to stitch,

help immediate.
Back not wrenched
face not scraped
teeth not chipped
hands not ripped

pants not torn
nor sweater, nor purse, nor coat,
bladder was empty,
her stomach had breakfast.
In some essential small corner

all is well.

10/27/11

Considering

Sitting under a tree of heaven
under a lowering sky
wondering aloud what might leaven
my life, brighten the day,
lift inevitable pain away?

No answer came,
no insight or lightening bolt.
Except to breathe and keep on
showing up, do my best,
appreciate, notice, consider

being content.

11/8/11

The Greater Tuberosity

A crack in the greater tuberosity,
another body part named,
limitation measured by experience.

Sounds more like a peak encountered
climbing Mount Everest, but in fact is
the ball atop the upper arm bone, the humerus,

that fits into the elegant shoulder socket
allowing movement in all directions,
magnificent and taken for granted,

until lost that is,
until healed
then gratitude.

11/8/11

Follow-Up, Dr. Jason K.

Bone bruised he said
cracked, no displacement

torn rotator cuff
but partial, not full.

Astounding he said
about the swift progress.

Magnificent range of motion
so soon after that kind of fall,

I feel certain you will
fully recover he said.

All these words soaking in,
setting out the desired pattern

as I am following
my own direction.

Keep on doing whatever you are doing,
perhaps start a little rehab,

not do more than is comfortable,
giving permission to listen

to the body speaking,
as I have learned to anyway.

Worth the wait, they said
while we all waited in the waiting room.

I've been seeing him
1 year (or 7 years), they said.

I tell everyone about him,
he's the best, they said.

Even late, he did not rush
still gentle, human, kind,

still thorough, skilled, considerate,
choosing to help, energy warm, transparent.

A healer by choice,
a doctor by training.

11/9/11

To Hammer

Love to hammer
to make noise
the immediacy
of pounding in a nail
of fixing something
making something

creation in action.
The heft of the hammer
in right hand.
I was the only one
who took a hammer to college
just in case.

I still have it
small, useful
scarred by the years.
Other heavier hammers
more impressive
and powerful came along

but the beauty of that first one….
Now joints and bones
can no longer absorb the hits
without a murmur.
My serious hammering days are over.
I may allow a tap, tap

to put up a picture
nail the hanger into soft drywall.
But not arm ricocheting off
unyielding hardwood.

If I am smart
those days are over.

11/17/11

Returning to the Scene

of the fall or near enough
to feel the aftershocks.

Apprehension
without comprehension,
heart fast, breath shallow,

feel ill, as if....
Takes weeks to understand the antidote:
Walk the street of the accident

to neutralize the fear
permeating the city air.
Each visit less vulnerable,

until moments might pass
of near normal buoyancy, resilience.
Until each time stepping out of the car

not envision falling...falling...
helpless to stop...
and then the pain, and partial blindness.

11/24/11

For Barbara and Me
In Some Ways in the Same Boat

How did we get so fragile,
we who had been indestructible?
Days passed from then and
we got older (though not yet old)
and accumulation of events,
choices made, conscious or unconscious,
wear and tear on the machinery,
countless sleepless nights,
stuff picked up from somewhere or someone
like barnacles on the hull of an ocean-going vessel.

In a blink
all those heavy days
bore down on us.
The lack of consistent self-care
as we cared for family, home, career,
as we worried about the future
pouring all—or more than
what we had—into...
keeping it all going.

Now, here we are,
not at the end,
but in sight,
still the possibility of healthful vigor
if only we could turn the corner,
get something elusive back
or follow some new insight,
the wisdom we've absorbed
used on our own behalf to

fill the empty places,
illuminate the dark spaces,
give us the chance
to do still, what we came to do:
be loving
be joyful
be a good example.

12/3/11

Abrupt Clarity

When I said
I give up on writing
I meant it.

And I meant
I give up on struggle
it is too hard

and I meant it
when I said
it is sad, but not devastating,

not the end of the world
just all I had been building.

You took it to mean
what it used to mean
coming from my old lips

and cautioned reflection
and wanted to change my mind
or calm my thinking.

But
I was right,
what is past is done

as far as setting out
my unsustainable future,
it is too hard

and I am giving up
on hard in my life.

Does this mean
I will not put words to page?
apparently not, for here they are

again,
restlessly leading me on.
And when the call came
last night at 3AM
and I thought my son

was wandering lost
in the cold, too far for my help,
there was an abrupt clarity

about what is important to me,
what I can do and not do,
what I have to let go.

12/12/11

Startling Starlings
Everett Road west of Riverwoods

In the middle of a murmuration
landscape and sky covered by wings
myriad dark apparently separate bodies
climb and swoop and soar in evident synchrony,
how can that be? Mysterious symphony
immersed in all that majestic energy
a blessing particularly chosen for me.

12/14/11

Intoxication of Hope

What kept me awake last night?
No, not caffeine ingested late
but hope, the possible solution
to an insurmountable problem
piled on all the others,
painful, worsening, at the core of everything.

The evident solution was obvious,
easy even, now clearly seen.
It may be only a direction to head
not the final steps,

or it may be the longed for, prayed for
answer to everything
or this one vital energy-zapping crucial thing...
intoxicating.

2012

1/1/12

Remembering a Little Girl

A little girl looks out
Grandma's picture window
at the frozen puddle-ponds
in neighboring winter fields.

Gets thickly dressed for outside:
snowpants, jacket, hat, mittens, boots, scarf
tied across nose and mouth
only blue eyes exposed.

Heads directly to the ice
stamping it to shards
mud underneath coats her red boots.
Tramps back to the country house

"Let me in, I'm cold" in her small girl voice.
"No, you only just got out"
after 30 minutes of getting her dressed.
She shuffles down the garage cement steps

with the locked door to the basement
at the bottom, she pokes the dead
crisp beetles and June bugs with a stick
interested in everything.

1/13/12

If Then Yes

If with every poem or most
I must somehow prove
I am literary
I can't...or won't

write as if to please.
But if I write every word
dripping saturated
with my personal honey,

my human divinity,
then yes,
I will breathe you in
and linger long and

I will write a song
just for you.

1/28/12

The Signature
To Eric Whitacre with gratitude

The beauty of dissonance,
in itself...and resolving,
the strength of moving to
and off of and onward,

continuing the run, each note
clear and strong, not shy away from
close connection,
let all notes be possible together

in the greater scheme of things.
Regardless of what was taught
about what was right or right rules once
in the world as it existed then.

To let become and bloom
from sheer joy of breath and sound
as if the world is being
created all over again...

as indeed it is...
from pure vibration.

2/22/12

Waiting at the Mini Car Repair

I thought it was an eye
but it was light on a mirror
on a car or plane or really a picture
half-blocked by a pole

caught out of a corner of a
quick glimpse and filled in
by that primitive part of the brain
that is always scanning for danger.

3/10/12

To Welcome the New
Thank you, Geary

Talk to the mesh he said,
truth I recognized.
I had not deliberately welcomed,
nor delicately integrated a new part of me,
inserted to keep the insides in
and the outsides out and
stave off potential (and more immediate)
death by intestinal strangulation.

The body from the first
may have snubbed, reacted against
what was supposed to be helpful,
and clearly now was in an uneasy truce of sorts,
neither side happy with what cannot be undone.
So how about we begin again.
Hello, I'm Margaret, your host, and you are?

"Meredith, Meredith the Mesh." *OK.*
What to do about this standoff?
"Evacuate the soldiers,
cells designed to repel invaders,
intolerant by nature and function."
Envisioning. Talk to the troops:

We need to find a rapprochement,
not mere accommodation, but surrender
to circumstance beyond our immediate control,
welcoming, whole-hearted acceptance.
Integration until mesh is me
and we are one...again.
Are you with me on this!?

"Of course, dear leader,
we'd follow you anywhere!"
Withdraw troops, disarm weapons.
Relearn hospitality, kindness, generosity.
Invite fear to tea,
you will see…you will see…
believe me.
We are creating the new reality.
Calm the waters.
Feed peace back into the loop.
All is well, I tell you.
All is well.

Talk to the mesh he reminded,
it's something you would do,
resolving conflict between
what *is* and *is not* you,
allowing, discerning, welcoming
what is new, come to help support you.

Stop struggling, holding on to pain,
to loss, to trauma, unforgiving,
unforgetting, if quiet for a moment
still lingering, still rejecting,
unwelcoming, unhealed.

Turn each mesh particle
into a haven for my cells
a harbor both necessary and lovely
as muscle grows into lattice
and scars resolve amicably,
advantage taken of symmetry,
embracing the possibility
of restored harmony.
All is well, I tell you
All is well.

3/16/12

Choosing Expansive
Spark #2

A door opens
walk through.
Opportunity knocks
answer.
A boat glides up to the dock
where you stand waiting
to take you to your dream
no explanations
no guarantees.
If you don't go
you will wonder
and if you don't go
what will you do
and if you don't...go
when will you find out
just what you are made of
just what you could be
if only?

3/17/12

Inspired

My mother has endured
repeated injections into her good eye
rounds of infections in one part or another
with eventual antibiotics and recovery.
The loss of sight, strength, and clarity
(still retaining the ability to talk to me).
Pain has dwelled in her joints and muscles
deep restorative sleep eludes her
a whole litany of diagnoses
yet she remains with us
and even cheerful sometimes.
If she can do that, I can do this
live each day as if it were the last...
and the next....

3/19/12

Monday Call

How calming to speak with her still,
how heart full,

wide-ranging, lots of laughing,
though words get lost

and threads of conversation sometimes.
To be on the other end of the line

talking, how ordinary.
How extraordinary!

And sometime looking back
the second gift...remembering.

To see my life, my work
through her generous eyes

the unfailing encouragement,
her unflagging support.

3/30/12

Broken Shoulder
True memory

I spared you from my tears.
Because you didn't see my pain

and I healed more quickly than most
(I am a healer and work at it),

now you say, it was not that bad
to crack and bruise the bone, tear the ligaments.

You forgot every gasp when I put on my coat,
the hour it took every day to get dressed.

How putting away glasses from dishwasher to shelf
I had to set them first on the countertop,

turn and use the other arm, the less injured one,
to raise each glass to the cabinet.

You were not with me in the shower
as I cried trying to wash my hair.

You generously let me have the main bed
and so you do not remember the restless longing for sleep

as I twisted to find some position that gave relief.
No, it all looked easy apparently,

no heavy drugs to dull the pain and give credibility.
You forgot the sheen of shock-sweat

as I struggled to stay conscious and lost parts of my vision,
my first-ever ambulance ride, better once horizontal.

You were reassured by my good humor in the ER,
evidently unaware of the effort behind the graceful dance,

my love.

4/11/12

Somewhere in the Middle More Towards the End
The Guides speak

Again they said
she will not listen
We will have to
knock her flat
no breath to breathe in
her heart pounding in
irregular rhythm
All this to just get her attention
get her to stop and listen

The days are short
the hours longer
when the body
minds not being younger
the mind not yet
beginning to wander
This window of opportunity
this sliver of eternity
all yours
if you pay attention

Don't piss it all away
this time

4/20/12

Baby Robins

Tiny bits of camouflage fluff
with tiny yawping contrast mouths
in a feathered bowl of twigs and grass
in a branch-crook of a white pine
needle-covered, near a bedroom window
in a house overlooking.

On a cold day in April
warmed by a broad feathered red breast
incessantly fed by both parents
protected, nurtured, and nourished
to someday...
fly.

5/2/12

In the Rain: Randolph St., Chicago

Colored lights
in stripes on
rain-slick pavement.

Red and green and
marquee white
enhanced by

encroaching night.
Catch the vision
between swipes

of the wiping blade
look between drops and
snap a shot that

sees what I see,
through the eye
through the lens

trapped in a black box
retrievable again.
Mistakes risked

imperfect attempts
the thrill of hopefulness
temporary though it is.

5/6/12

Reborn at 60

Moonlight like
frost on the grass,
biggest and brightest
sky-face of the year,
the perigee moon,
product of off-center
elliptical orbit
and earth-centered
point of view.

Apparent full moon
to turn 60 to,
the dark lit
celestial celebration
and I am
lighthearted in relief
somehow as if
the rest of days are
skiing downhill,
the burden lifted.

As if the bones
have sufficiently melted,
muscles gone to mush,
to now begin rebuilding
from the bottom up,
incorporating wisdom
and all that means.
I do my part
but the rest is
not up to me,
therein the relief.

The rest, the outcome,
the product of labor,
all that I am expressed,
and I am not in control.
That unbearable weight is gone
and I am left with
joyful levitation...
unexpected happiness,
blissful hopefulness.
Amen...again.

5/14/12

Monday Conversation

When I thought she was gone,
no more conversations with her voice now worn,
tears coursed down cheeks unbidden
and when she at last answered the phone,
flooded this time with relief.

For someday soon will be the day
there is no answer or
a call will come to say she has
slipped from this realm
to ever-after.

Let her go.
Not a matter of whether
but when,
one more day, we have one more.

6/3/12

Being

I am lying in bed
on soft sheets of cotton
empty but for this thought
aware for a long moment
like on Pramod's balcony
when times were thin
sipping her tea
imagining.

6/14/12

From Eric, Prada, Crystal, and Others

To be fully
yourself
to hit that
moving target
keep going
keep growing
keep glowing,
to remain essential
yet expansive
inviting others in
but unconcerned.
Who are you,
why are you here?
Not to dwell on
the obvious
but what are you
good at
what calls you
or heals you?
What fills you
with almost unbearable
joy?

Do that
Be that
Don't settle

6/18/12

Living in the Present Tense
Lunch at King Maa restaurant

No longing, no regrets
no guilt over what was or wasn't.

Here, spearing the last
cube of chicken from my plate

viola playing in my ear
piano accompaniment

sun, blue sky, wisp clouds at fringe
cars drive by, people walking

from the mirror behind
to the glass beside

disappearing behind the mirror ahead.
Yellow daylilies, green spike leaves

royal blue Mini (mine)
with white racing stripes and top

a wren in the tree of heaven
cool inside, hot outside

glass of water, ice clinking.

Breath out
breath in

heart beats in even rhythm
eyes open, pen moving

this one moment...
this one moment.

6/23/12

The Penultimate Visit

One last thing you have to teach me:
how to let you go,
though you are gone from form,
knowing you are never far from me,
your beloved daughter.

So little of you left here,
no detailed conversation,
bits and fragments of memory
unreliably told with words

that don't quite fit
the meaning you struggle for.
But your face has the familiar expressions,
your eyes the same blueberry blue,

an occasional smile crosses your lips
as I sit near to you.
Hands and arms black and blue
from blood drawn or IVs,
remnants of the last hospital stay.

They say you are better
than you were and
I have to believe them,
but much more is gone

since our last conversation.
Now and then your awareness, and with it
sorrow of loss (better to not know),
and the apology so heartfelt,

"Oh, Margaret Mary, I am so sorry."
What to say to that, heart breaking?
Keep moving, ask a simple question:

"Do you want more water?"
"How do you like it here?"
"Is the food OK?"
"The people seem nice."

To all but the first
I cannot understand (or translate)
a lucid answer.
Maybe her words mean something

or maybe not.
Her eyesight is shot,
her hearing minimal,
also her sense of smell.

The cues that could keep her
tied to coherence missing
even on a good day,
where are we then

on the cusp of evaluation?
What life to medicate her for
(with what painful side effects)?
At what point (this one?)

to say let us call in hospice?
Find support for her and us,
give comfort, knowing
this is the end?

To have seen her,
held her ice cold hands,
worth traveling any distance,
any heartbreak, any amount of tears.

It is not
whether you will pass on,
but when,
and sooner more likely than later.

What we do with this time,
what opportunities taken
to heal, to wish well,
this is the final gift bestowed.

7/2/12

After Kip (No Singing)

It is as if
her whole complex
85 year life of

memories and actuality is
broken up into
4 word phrases,

shaken in a lotto wheel,
and a phrase selected
more or less at random,

occasionally matching
the conversation.
Mostly she is unaware now,

but occasionally she will notice
and apologize
breaking my heart all over.

What I would wish
for her is peace
and she has more a measure of this.

Her life here lingers
losing a bit, then another bit,
until we have lost all of it.

7/2/12

The Children Are Watching

to see how we handle this

...grieving.
What we do or not,

that they would choose
to safely feel.

Watching to be sure
we are OK,

don't vanish, crushed
under the weight of it.

Learn from us to trust
even darkness.

7/3/12

Cactus Flower

First bloomed at full moon.

From the single bud a sudden opening,
white petals wide and luminous.

How long to last...unknown.

15 years gestation,
open under moonlight,
hidden with the sun.

7/13/12

AM

She is quiet
she is still
she is peaceful

she is getting ready
to walk the long tunnel
ever grace-filled.

7/13/12 PM

Gratitude as an Antidote to Grief
For Dorothy

Grief as a tidal wave
after the tsunami
washing lives out to sea.

Roots ripped out
of living trees,
no end to sorrow.

But to be grateful
for what is and was,
even as future is lost

to notice and bless
peace and stillness
in place of struggle.

To hope for music
and music comes,
to imagine comfort

of holding a hand,
singing a childhood song,
praying a familiar prayer,

to desire someone to act as if
I were there,
and it is done.

Blessings on everyone.

8/19/12

Grief and the Heart

To be broken-hearted
not just as metaphor

to be broken-hearted
with loss so uprooting

the heart cannot keep on
its invisible beating

in rhythm set at birth—
or before, really—

with the embedded pattern
of the mother's heart within

the fetal rapidness.
Yes, it makes sense

as much as anything
that once the mother's heart stops

her child might
drown in the silence.

8/26/12

Gorecki: Symphony of Sorrowful Songs
Thanks for the link, Eric Whitacre

In the stillness
non-essentials fall away
light shines in darkness.

Life is rebuilt
from mostly reused bricks
previously battered down.

In the shadows
music builds for those
with patience to listen

to beauty becoming.
Those who trust long enough
to invest the time

who will breathe with
ascending notes, climb the mountain
be washed clean

come back down to life
transmuted water to wine
and back again.

Intoxication.
Dedication
to feeling.

The Phoenix rising
from everyday ash
willing.

In the end
a shift in key
a point of light toward

the hoped for
healed reality.

8/29/12

Jean McGrew Crosses the Bridge
Call from her daughter

So I did hear after all
when Jean heard the call
and left this life

as she lived it,
on her own terms,
with spunk and clarity,

family gathered round
for the last peaceful breath,
comforted by their mutual faith.

I miss her encouragement,
optimism, healing words, determination,
contagious inspiration, poetry, good humor,

writing to her heart or liver,
envisioning Monet's bridge at Giverny
to cross over the ocean back to health,

her talks at the library, wellness and senior centers
complete with healing basket of props,
poems, stories, heartfelt collections,

compassion, support, persistence.
Our lunches at Hackney's in Lake Zurich.
Miss you, rare kindred spirit!

Inevitable I reach an age
where my mothers are gone
and gone and gone and

I am left
mothering
on my own.

"We are always close
in heart and spirit,"
she last wrote to me.

8/31/12

Medication
And not struggling

Each pill
a little boat

like the man in the flood
as water rises to his roof
who says he will wait
and be saved by the Lord,
but gives up rescue
by the rowboat,
speedboat and helicopter,
drowning in his faith,
ignoring what heaven sent.

I am trying to pay attention
not get stuck in
a rigid box of belief

knowing I don't know
what is the right path

and what I knew
for certain sure

has changed like water
changes shape

no matter the glass or
vase or bucket or pot
poured into.

9/6/12

Reading *Garment of Shadows* by Laurie R. King

I couldn't see myself
on the other side of darkness
you lose a mother only once

what is broken cannot be fixed
what reassurance
could be offered
what meaning or strength

found in contemplating healing?
It is as if I woke with amnesia
unaware of who I am

clues all around of someone
who lived where I lived
and worked and was a friend

but who she is now
or who might know
or what road to follow…?

In the meantime…
sun rises…sun sets
the day is sunny or gray

put one foot in front of the other
the nights blending together
I dream in language I do not understand.

9/13/12

For STM

I want to save you
from the brushfire of grief
jumping the firebreak

in the space between us.
Yet there is no true safety,
no way to know what will ignite,

the past dark tucked away
somewhere deliberately to survive.
Now the door opens

and oxygen feeds the fire
and you are alight
with your own grief unresolved.

Who is to say
what heals, what harms,
how much trust is involved,

how much patience?

10/2/12

Those Times

Sometimes life
can flatten you
until you are
a molecule thin
and then
further flatten
until bone is not
connected to bone

and muscle, and
brain ceases to function.
Until what was you
is dispersed so widely
and broadly
over time and space
and evolution
with no chance

of recognition
or resolution.
What could have been
cannot be
or even be imagined.
Then you have to stop,
what choice do you have.
Stop and begin again.

10/16/12

Three Months Out

There is a sweetness to grief
a purity with no resolution
clarity without recourse

as the days wear on
and the mother is gone
the photos notwithstanding.

Sometimes unexplained
pressure on the bed at night
as if someone is sitting on the covers.

Sometimes still
the unbearable shoulder-weight
but more often than not

life continues
and even laughter
and appreciation of fall color.

Days may pass in forgetfulness
until a trigger: a smell of roses
a random thought about cashews

or the color turquoise.
A snap on a jacket, a fragment of on old song
an especially juicy Michigan peach.

And memory rushes back
and guilt almost
and cleansing tears of course

as what was flattened
re-inflates and
what was dormant
reanimates.

A bald kindness to grief
sympathy without mercy
gratitude for feeling something

while flailing in the dark
grasping for some thread to follow
gasping for enough air to sustain.

11/25/12

Evening Walk

There was a time not long past
when what I longed for was to walk
left and right leg muscles strong in balance

no thought required to lift each foot
to walk like everyone else.
Now I have that,

in all the other ruckus it slipped in
as other essential organs declined
taking all the attention.

No limp that I can feel
just left-right, left-right
foot falls even, no slap on pavement.

Now it is bones and heart, kidneys and lungs
drawing all intention.
Muscles willing to strengthen

to carry me, to lift me up even.

11/29/12

Grief Report—Four Months Out

I don't think of her
every minute or even every day,
she pops into thought unexpectedly,
often not a sad memory,
sometimes the gasp of a stab.

Days and nights mostly normal to report.
If there are problems they seem
unrelated to grief,
not caused or exacerbated by it.
Even the clear image of her lying on satin,

crystal rosary in bony folded hands,
wrinkles of pain smoothed out by the process,
acceptance, a little teary
if not held in mind too long.

Grieving is not linear and cannot be measured
by day to day progress on a graph.
It is sporadic and variable,
each day or hour its own kind of survival,
another release of control.

12/4/12

Another Sister with Cancer

It is good Mom is gone
for this surely would have killed her:

breast cancer for her last untouched
and youngest daughter.

Now all four beloved daughters with cancer
one gone young, two past it, one beginning the fight.

Of the three boys
each with their own particular struggles:

stones, inner demons, paralysis,
the youngest nearer than the others to death.

Yes, all this with the rest, would have been
too great a burden to bear

for someone for whom
her children were most everything.

12/17/12

Permission to Myself
After Newtown

I cannot allow myself
to be heartbroken again

(and my mind remembers
my son, my daughter in kindergarten).

I've been down that road
and know where it leads

and it helps no one.
The heart shuts down and the breathing

and without immediate intervention...well....
So, some things kept hidden, maybe temporarily.

The cupboard opens and risk a peek in
and if there is enough resilience

then open a little more,
the eventual goal, complete exposure.

But if a tiny crack open is too much
and tears begin to roll down,

step back, close for now,
stay here with me, dear one,

stay here. Time enough to heal
as you will. So much in the stew pot

bubbling over hot onto the stove.

12/22/12

Evening Walk

Sun descending I am walking west
gentle slope to the frozen pond.

Going east, a slender man in striped parka
yellow, red, black, with black pants and cap

sleek black dog on a red leash.
Both quiet in the cold

stop to watch two white-tailed deer
disguised by deeper shadows

of the trees in front of
the empty farmhouse.

A gray squirrel runs down an elder oak
another eats perched on a lower branch.

Duck or crow sound
distressed or angry.

Open sky overarched with
streaming clouds of apricot or rose

alternating with unlikely strips of robin's egg blue
backdrop to elegant leafless branches

luminous light glows over everything.
Oh, Holy Night.

12/25/12

Sliced by a Mandoline

Your fingertip to my fingertip
not as I'm used to it
while attached to bone,

but the tip alone, a bit of nail—
like a dot of pancake batter
on a granite counter—on its own.

Put in a bag
place on ice
send it off
to be reattached or not.

Wait at home
on my own
for the son to call
did the bleeding stop?

Turn the oven back on,
put the roast beef back in.
Resume Christmas
with all the trimmings
as if…

we knew
what is truly valuable.

12/29/12

Past Dusk Walk
First snowfall

Concentrate
on staying upright.

No frozen dog tracks
no shiny new cyclone fence

enclosing a house yet unbuilt.
No large lit white brick house

impressive with white twinkling lights
two massive paneled white wood doors

with two big plumed wreaths with huge pine cones.
Stop to look up at

three honking geese in a line flying east.
No visible sunset turning sky to rose

just gray clouds turning to darker gray
turning to night black.

No blue and green, red and yellow
lights reflecting in the re-freezing snow-melt.

Concentrate on staying upright
walking home on into the night.

2013

1/2/13

For My Son
Who Is Leaving

Did my mother sometimes watch me
doing things the hard way
and not say anything to discourage?

Now I know silence can mean support,
silence can mean neglect, silence can be
the best one can do, silence can mean I love you

and trust you to make your own mistakes,
find your own unique learning way
which often may not be mine.

Then there you stand, young but grown
while I was not looking and so much I did not know
and hug for as long as we both can hold on.

1/4/13

Evening Walk Series
Fully present and noticing

Amber light slants later and later.
Man in all black walks like a boxer,
hood up, hands tucked into sleeve ends,

down the block and farther.
Tracks on snow-covered frozen pond

together, then separate end to end.
Wind picks up conversation

of two men laying lines to dig
the hole of a house yet unbuilt.

One man in long camel dress coat
holding the plans, the other in work clothes

planting pegs in icy ground,
steam shovel at the ready, still now.

Boy and girl hand-in-hand self-absorbed,
walking a dog smaller than a Shepherd.

She wears a maroon ski-band with a gold "M."
"Hi" and "Hi" back, passing on the path.

Gold filters through pin oak leaves to salt box bricks
curtains open to an empty dark dining room.

Half orange sun rests on rooftops then sets in the west
orange blush smears on the horizon
one unexpected slice caught on the ash treetops.

1/8/13

Walking Series: January Thaw

Difference of night and day
walking down the gently sloping way

loud hum of generator motor
tapping of the bricklayer

sizing his bricks, cigarette held by lips
male voices down making a cement basement form.

No deer, no squirrels, no birds, no dogs,
mud tire tracks on the asphalt.

Noon sun shines on the stippled ice pond,
water rising where footprints had been.

1/9/13

John is Dying They Say

My baby brother now grown
is dying and I don't know why.
Why I am here and healed
and he is suffering
preparing to leave

    unless it is
to crack our hearts open
just that much more.
And what we do with that
remains...

    infusing everything.

1/10/13

Trusting I Will Know

If I were a sculptor
which I am and
my material was flesh and bone

the day to day mundane,
what would I...have I...
shaped of this thus far?

Chipping away non-angel slivers
molding with not always nimble fingers
trust and hope and in despair

keep on shaping...shaping...trusting
I will know what is too much,
what is enough.

1/12/13

Saturday Walk 5PM

Solitary
great blue heron stands still
at thinning gray dusk
in the middle of the pond

visible only from a sliver angle
otherwise unseen
in shadows and reflections
of trees on water skimming the ice.

Needle-nose beak like compass needle
barely moves to the south
away from the sloping road.
Air from early temperate to late freezing.

Sun sinks without hint of a trace.

1/18/13

Wake for My Brother

What a strange thing
your body lying there
not the right color face
not you animating from inside

not anywhere or maybe
found everywhere, I can still
hear your voice
and know what it took to leave us.

Yet here we all are
gathered...you would have loved it.
Not the sorrow, but surely
appreciate the memory of laughter.

1/18/13

1964-2013

The youngest of "the boys"
and first to go.
Packed it all into 49 years.
What is undone, remains undone.

Yes, regret a bit,
guilt a bit for not being perfect,
taking each opportunity to talk,
but I am human and finite

and you, now infinite.
So much of what I remember
was early on, most photos
unfamiliar—even if I was in them.

The "what if onlys"…
not helpful, but inevitable.
In hours, the funeral mass,
but you know all this.

What is done is done,
what is undone remains undone,
but all is most certainly forgiven.
Time to gather, grieve and continue on.

1/18/13

Prayer of Intercession

Your face so young,
so much I didn't know,
how far you traveled,
not often to see me.

No complaints now,
nor pain and suffering.
Glad Mom went first,
was there waiting for you

'cause this would have killed her sure.
Not for us, only one in deep trouble,
another waits uncertain fate,
new scars and pain and hard things,

loss and growth and opportunity.
I cannot think of what eventuality.
Be there for her I plead:
Watch out for your sister.

Do not wait with the others
over there to welcome her.
Envision her lungs, her bones as clear.
Breathe healing life energy

over and in and around and through
permeating every cell of her willing body.

1/19/13

Funeral Night

Buried now
in the cold ground
surrounded by familiars.

No more waiting,
the other shoe has dropped
and that is that.

What it was all for
I cannot begin to imagine,
the effects of one short life

ripple out and ripple out,
interwoven, interacting,
mistakes made, choices chosen.

Now or tomorrow
what we do with all that
to change next time

or do again,
hopefully not real soon.
"We have to stop meeting like this."

1/20/13

Finished Later

Long streams of clouds
stack up like
white caps approaching the shore
and I remember what was
and is nevermore.

Remember what I left
and what I left for
all written in the clouds
all backed by the sky-blue
memories, I remember you.

1/23/13

Resolution of Darkness

It is nature
for dark to roll around
once a day, an exception
being extreme geography.

The mottled darkness
of closed eyelids,
and shadows deep and shallow,
total dark of the depths of the ocean

where some adapted creatures
still live and thrive.
It is nature
for sun to resume each morning,

even if clouds blanket the sky
light gets through.
Even in nighttime
shine stars and moon.

So it is not hopeless
to wait it out,
the globe revolving as it does
and me standing on the surface

the merest micro-dot and
the center of the universe.

1/26/13

Momentary

A solitary orange sparkle
on thin veneer of fresh snow

from a sliver of setting sorbet sun
through skeletal tree branches

catching an ice crystal
just so

2/1/13

Appearance Can Deceive

Such a fine line
between sad and calm

the face may even
look the same

while inside
heart is breaking.

Not broken like a china cup
dropped from a height to the hard floor,

the shattered fragments scattered.
Heart slivers do not separate from each other

and have to be glued to mend
never quite as beautiful whole again.

But broken heart like each beat is heavy
each beat is hard, not easy

like every living cell in the body
looking forward cannot see

like every cell looking back
cannot bear it.

In the center, the moment,
apparently still in the eye of the storm

there may be the appearance
of calm.

2/1/13

Grief-Stricken

Sitting here
I can hear
soap bubbles pop in the sink
and warm air rushing through the vent

Hyper aware
and skinless-raw
and on some plane somewhere
alright

2/1/13

Metastases

Draw a skeleton on a blackboard
each bone indelible true and clear

and with chalk mark
each errant dot growing there.

Erasable.

2/5/13

From Jerry de G

Painting with dew
how ephemeral, ethereal

to use what evaporates in sun
as a fluid medium

for pattern and rhythm.
Dew on grass

what could be more obvious
quickly preserved by photograph.

Use what is available in the moment
to express what can be expressed:

beauty and optimism and
hopefulness.

2/9/13

Saturday Backyard

In the thaw
the wind blew off
the frosting from the branches.

Shimmer of crystals
seen in sunlight
slanting across the fields.

Cold enough to still be winter
days now perceptibly longer,
palpable anticipation of spring.

Mild days turn as they will
no effort does it take, not even
awareness or remembering.

On the snow
tracks and shadow
evidence of all those passing.

2/23/13

Thinking of Dorothy

By all accounts
I should have been dead
several times over,

but here I am thriving
and there you have it.
Dire predictions like

long-term weather maps,
unreliable as a crystal ball
looking into a shadow future.

If you ask, as you might,
what I did to skid sideways
off the path leading to the cliff

I would say…a lot and…
I don't know. Begin by believing
through a sliver of a crack it is possible.

Not necessary to have no doubt
but hold kindness in your heart
allow hopeful to take root.

Heal whatever rises to the surface
of your perceptive awareness
even those things, especially those things

that seem un-healable,
wounds that have festered raw,
anger like concentrated acid

it would seem impossible
to ever neutralize.
With support you draw to you,

the love and nascent forgiveness
for yourself first,
the aggressive array of seed cells

scattered like a sneeze into bones
can melt away like snowflakes
on a summer sidewalk,

a memory with no hold over you.
"There are no guarantees. But
expect the result to be better

than you could possibly imagine."
Find your way I pray….
Stay

3/2/13

The House on Cadieux

In my mind the girl
with the long blonde ponytail
and the loping dog on a leash

is always there jogging past
the classic colonial on the corner
that I saw once at dusk after a funeral

when it was cold but not snowy.
You were eager to show
and tell us what you imagined

your life could be living there,
what would certainly change
what would stay the same.

Unknowing, you
had circled back to the town
your great-great grandfather farmed in

once upon a time
when life was no less risky
and choices laid out plain.

3/3/13

Stronger than You Think

Make something of what happens
not just a victim passively flattened.

Knocked down, get up
wind knocked out, re-inflate.

In the dark
the seed of light

a path to follow out.
Follow it.

3/4/13

Too Many Shoes

Waiting for the other shoe to drop
how many feet can there be?

If you love...
to bear the loss

as shoe after shoe after shoe
falls to earth.

More still...
and more still

inevitable
as breathing

or blinking
or heart beating.

To remember the gift seed
in the dark days.

Each loss revealing...
the choice:

to make the most
of time.

3/12/13

For My Baby Sister

Perhaps the tide has turned
with this one surprising test result.
The unrelenting unbroken string of bad news

snapped and from now on *(I whisper)*
although an uphill climb
redemption is guaranteed.

Oh, I would vote for that!
I would put in my coin,
I would leave my heart unarmored

and risk it all again.
Not to save you,
but to keep you here

to have those sister talks
and laugh until we pee.
Laugh and remember

and cry sometimes.
And that last hug
is not the last hug

and we walk on together
for a long time still
hand in hand as always.

3/14/13

Return

More birds than there were
not heard for months here

the songs loud enough to penetrate
brick and glass

calling, calling to each other.
Did you make it ok?

How was the flight?
Want to grab some breakfast?

3/14/13

Take Care

It has been suggested
and it seems right
to cry more
let out the tight muscles
deplete the pool of unshed tears
let the water flow...flow
release the pressure don't you know.

To sleep to dream
let the inward screams dim
in the prevailing calm.
To breathe
not the shallow barely air in
but down to the toe tips if I can.
Laughing and bubbles are well and good
but mixed in, not what
I *should* do to take care
but what I *could*.

3/18/13

Grateful

No one right way
to heal.
No one size fits all
or for all time.

To be present and aware
and loving,
forgiving what can be,
and re-visiting.

Fill the heart with grateful,
breathe in grateful
for each small thing
noticing.

For each talk,
each easy breath,
each pain-free hour,
each tasty meal,
each soft fuzzy animal,

each day of sun or rain,
the moon shining again.
To show up…aware
for all the time you have
as much as it is…unknowable.

3/25/13

Phone Calls after Voice Lessons

I had parents who loved me
and though that didn't automatically make life easy
it made the unlikely a smidge more possible.

At this time last year and this time of day
and this place looking out at the church,
Mom and I were still talking as we could then
of life and news and goings on,

of thoughts and memories and connection.
I would describe the scene I saw
the squirrel or cardinal or kids playing on the grass,
the kinds of clouds, the oak downed in the storm,

what the grandkids were up to,
news I stored away through the week to share.
She would listen, her life much smaller now,

and occasionally laugh and interrupt
with news of her own, not so much medical
—my role was mostly apart from all that.

Good days and lesser days,
but none for us of bad days.
All the time together was enough...

and not enough.

Her mind would drift some
and my mouth would run-on some
and we would laugh then

and keep on talking for hours until
lunch or appointments or a knock at her door
spelled the end of that one.

Knowing, though unspoken,
at some point seen in a closing distance,
one talk would be the last.

Knowing I would be left here bereft,
knowing I would write it out
and ride it out and remember…

a kind of immortality, to call her back to me.

4/4/13

Coming to Terms
After Roberta

Coming to terms with
something buried
something risen to the surface.

Allowing the numb to thaw
meandering through the forest
not entirely aimless

above the winding river
cutting through the rock
over jagged mountaintops

ragged breath in discovery
of what lay behind, what waits ahead.
A gasp, a whisper, a feather brush

is all it takes to erase the bookmark
of traumatic events lodged in the gut
preventing ease and possibility.

Forgiveness, perspective, re-frame
the scene, seen from a perch above…
and in the telling to a gentle witness

the possibility of sweet release.

4/4/13

Written at the Bahia Resort

It does not do
to list all the losses
as if there is a merit badge
given for exemplary grieving.

Or to talk about
all the steps taken
through shards of glass,
or to not talk
acting as if nothing
can penetrate the armor
or awaken the numb to feel.

It is just advised
to show up each day
pull out the splinters
that have worked
their way to the surface.
Heal from all of this
and go on healing.

4/9/13

Fear of Relaxation
Waiting for massage at Catamaran spa

To become too loose,
chain slipping out
of the sprocket.
Feet can't find purchase on pedals,
fear of forgotten gears.

A young woman passes by
with pen and paper,
words come and are saved
as if the bicycle still moves.
And it is fear forgotten.

Who am I without
taut tension on the wire?

5/1/13

For Comfort, Really

She came to tell me something
that even when she was gone
she would still be here with me.

And all the rest who once were here
would always be there,
the veil so thin between me and them.

Though no arms to hug back
or cheek to touch or hand to hold,
the rest of them, the essence of all of them,

still here…always.

So she was not missing them she said,
they seemed very close and present to her
and I knew she had at least one foot out the door.

She was not afraid mostly
so how could I be,
both clinging to our eternity.

5/7/13

First Egret of the Season

Stalk legs in water
stalk neck stretched out
smear of body mirrored beneath.

Still as a painting
brain so small
head is barely visible

like the point end of
a sharpened #2 pencil.
Watchful...

then folds back into
a swan-like form
gliding until

another potential fish
ripples on pond surface
neck stretches back out

...waiting.
No strike yet
nor prepare to fly.

One moment that is all.
I stop for one moment
in the middle.

5/15/13

Hope and Directions
Listening again to instrumental Water Night

Calm, a sliver
away from sorrow,
but the body
the mind
knows rest in one.

Shadows may be
respite...or darkness
lurking to jump out
no matter the security
of the neighborhood.

How to follow a line
back to peace
from grief expressed
I wish I could tell you,
but you know

there is a lifeline
to pull to shore
or crumbs you left behind
or someone nearby to
hold the vision of safety.

You will...and I will...
walk that line,
not together probably,
but sometime...
and return....

If death overtakes
someone close in the meantime
it is not their grim failure to outrun,

but inevitable close of a chapter
however grace-filled and long.

If you believe or consider
we all circle back in some mystery
then, as a circle has no end,
it is not yet over....

And if something stirs up
mud from the bed of the river
time will settle every large or small particle
gently to the bottom again
and clarity and calm will rule the realm.

5/17/13

Heart Instructions/Description
Begun in hospital...long night

Calm heart
quiet heart
gentle heart
kind heart

Whole-hearted
sweet heart
calm and quiet heart
forgiving heart

Non-judging heart
peaceful heart
good-hearted heart
smart heart

Healing heart
healed heart
consoling heart
grieving heart

Open-hearted
soft heart
quiet heart
steady heart

Sweet heart
singing heart
steady heart
rough and ready heart

Heart furnace
transforming heart
heart core
sound heart

to the heart of darkness
and back out again

Healthy heart
whole heart
smart heart
calm heart

Sweet heart
held in The Hands
cradled in them
protected from

bruising
from anything
untoward and
less than…

Good heart
my own heart
my own good heart
reliable heart…

on and on
in calm heart rhythm…

5/23/13

To Unravel Mystery

I can't tell you
why I woke with heart

racing in the night.
I would like to

understand and avoid
what I can control

to protect tender
essential organs.

Though I can reason back
or remember, write a list of context,

reassure myself with such like,
somewhere I know

what things are unknowable,
what mystery blinds me.

Still I must sleep again
and wake and choose to live.

5/23/13

Not Looking Ahead Exactly

I don't know how to do this
I said not whining,

tears running down both cheeks.
I don't think I can grieve

and process loss of this
multiplicative magnitude.

One added to another,
and to many others,

with another looming.
How can I bear to watch

to witness, to be present,
to allow feelings,

not to numb into oblivion
by any possible means?

I am me, and who I am is
strong from years of training,

and somehow grace is found,
and somehow we will make the most

of the time we have.
Heal from, learn from…even this.

5/23/13

Nearing Anniversary
For STM

I might tell you
what I remember
from 40 years ago

and though you were there
and we were simpatico
your memories may not be

even recognizable to me,
either morphed over time,
put through that gauze sieve

we each have
or true from your point of view,
but maybe the image

has blurred or completely erased
and what mattered to me
enough to file away

just vanished from your life story.
Or we each remember bits
and piece together say, that date the first summer

when we were supposed to go to a horse show
but ended up making out on the beach.
Maybe you remember the color and make of the borrowed car

or where we went for dinner after
and both of us recall the unexpectedly cold wind
blowing off the lake, the threat of rain,

and I remember the insistence of your lips on mine
as we made our tent under the sandy blanket
and my passionate body awakened for the first time

like an iron slowly heating up to red hot
not an incandescent bulb you could turn on or off,
the abandon of desire almost scaring me with intensity.

5/24/13

Yesterday's Walk

I go to the pond
because the sky is blue
and temperature's cool.

No egret today nor otter
no mallard pair nesting
gliding or tails upending.

The pond is presence,
reflecting the plain gray block house
with more beauty than reality.

Small circle ripples
appear from fish mouths or bugs
breaking surface tension.

Two young girls scootering,
one milk chocolate, one blonde,
both exuberant and strong.

Up and down the block they go, full speed
up and down, then switch to kid-sized bikes,
energy seemingly inexhaustible.

One has moved into the newest house
apparently now finished. A father makes a brief
appearance on the driveway to check up.

In their own world for now.
One says Hi to me
I say back Hello.

5/29/13

Bedroom Window

What do sparrows know
of vagaries of wind—
effect yes, but not cause,
when it begins and ends—

both tiny feet
cling to a small branch
as it rolls from side to side
up and down, all around

finally resort to flight.

6/10/13

Antidote to Violence
Heidi from Turkey: Virtual Choir 4

"This will be our reply to violence: to make music more intensely, more beautifully, more devotedly than ever before."
Leonard Bernstein

Outside
on ordinary street
police brutality

Inside
hearts open
to harmony

one plus one plus...
out to not quite infinity
singing as inspiration

and free expression
without borders or boundaries
without preset limitation

The heart vibration
out through the throat
as antidote to violence

6/11/13

My Love,

To lay with you in a darkened room
nested like similar-sized spoons

just as we did once long ago
but still in memory, though

we are different than we were
older true, wiser in some ways.

To love and allow love to amplify and return
to dive into dark and repeatedly back again.

To believe it is worth
putting one foot in front of the other

over and over...and together
breathe out and breathe in

being in
this time we have.

6/15/13

Singer with the Rough Voice
From an interview on night radio

Grief sings with a voice
though not smooth is seductive

and hypnotically you fall asleep
to joy and sunlight on leaves,

drifting in a dark abyss
ultimately of your own making.

As you sleep, you can wake
at any moment you can say: enough.

And mean it this time.
Fill with fuel for what comes next

certain there is purpose, one step
beginning with now.

6/21/13

Aggressor

A half-size rabbit
sits on a cement step
chewing the edge of a grass-mat.

A ground squirrel undulates,
its stripes aquiver, assessing
territory from a safe distance.

A short stand-off.
Rabbit makes the first move,
a brief lunge forward as if to challenge

and squirrel scampers
not thinking
not risking.

6/23/13

Daily Pattern

Resistance to sleep
surely the day is not over
can squeeze a few more
drops of blood from the hours

until day is flipped with night
going to bed with first pale light.
With shorter day inevitably I say:
Surely the day is not over.

And repeat. And repeat
as if I am unaware of consequence
as if I cannot re-choose.
Both not true. Reset. Begin.

6/25/13

The Other Side of Rain

A line
in the road
I cross
while driving.

No not that one
not painted man-made
but on one side
wet

on one side
dry
with some degree
of precision

as if a cloud
had sharp edges
and no wind to blow
errant drops

as if rain fell
instantly and no longer
as if I came upon
something

just after a pulse and
before evaporation
blurred the line
before and after

something
at this precise
time...
noticing.

6/25/13

Not Up to Me

It is not up to me
you see
if the sun rises
or the moon falls
if rain remains
suspended as fog.

One day into the next
flies by or dawdles
snail slow.
I wouldn't know
where to even begin.

That is good news—
the weight of the world,
whether healing or not,
at peace or at war—
not on my shoulders.
I can sit over here
and twiddle my thumbs

or dervish-dance
if I wish.
The conduct of matter
or people for that matter
whatever I might think or say,
not up to me.

What I *can* do
every single day
is *be*...present
generous-gracious
grateful-honest
loving-fearless.

6/29/13

Summer Night

No fireflies
then one
at the window
drawn to a light
too big to mean a mate

One, in this time
of biblical rains
not even a pair
matching flash to flash
dot to dash

7/1/13

MRI on Wed.
Sister

Yes, I spoke with her this evening
and yes, it was good for us to talk.

Hours we went on about everything
unfolding, spiraling deeper as time passed.

I cannot allow tears to flow now,
taking my own advice to her

to remember what is still unknown,
not jump ahead as if the worst.

Yet you know inside what you know,
and that is not as fixed as it seems,

and I know healing is possible.
Yes, even from this. And so

I will not give darkness a form,
invite the worst to be our reality

by speaking the words aloud
of what could be, if how it *feels*

is how it *is*. Let us take this week
remaining and wait suspended

but not unhappy, and find the things
that can give your life "quality"

for however long as may be.

7/12/13

Almost 1 Year Later
Marking July 14th. Thank you, Elizabeth Gilbert

Mom is dead,
she cannot die again.
The worst has happened,

in the past.
Not awaken every day
wondering if *this* is the day.

Release anxiety
like fluff in the air
from ripe dandelions,

like habits acquired
from practice or experience,
embedded in nerve nets

so deep-buried, impossible
to return to naiveté
until this one day

when one person may say:
it is in the past.
It cannot repeat. Release.

And like that,
one finger snap,
it is.

7/16/13

Virtual Choir 4
Watching screen shots by Elisabeth

To be seen,
to be seen singing,

to allow
sounds to emerge

and release,
to take the step

driven to connect
or belong or create

a tiny piece of beauty,
trusting.

To open heart
and mouth,

let energy go forth
melding with others

in the same quest,
hoping.

To strive and persist,
to learn and teach,

to wait for the outcome,
patient.

To join without boundaries,
to encourage, to support,

to accept grace and be
generous.

To demonstrate flight,
each a feather on a wing,

at least a little bit...
fearless.

7/22/13

Listening to and Reading Neil Gaiman

I would ask you how to do this,
but you wouldn't know how
to bring forth words out of my mouth,

only I can attempt the task,
take up the gauntlet laid down, and
only I might catch the "something"

that glints in the right kind of light,
seen casually out of the corner of one eye.
If I do catch it you will know,

you can't help really, though you can urge me on
from your distance and after-the-fact encourage.
If you do not like the result, but lie,

I will know, only the truth will do.
And *I* know and *you* know no poem
is for everyone, no novel, no story,

but...if it *is* for you
it could change everything...
be ready...for the eventual inevitable.

7/30/13

29th Birthday

Happy birth-giving day to me!
The son who was #1
making a mother of me,

as a baby did his job,
but the marathon of patience, trust, strength
and endurance fell mostly to me (and you)

appropriately enough during
the '84 Olympic opening ceremonies,
52 hours of labor and delivery.

Dark-haired, two-weeks-late sleepy boy...
surprise! Aided in the end
by gentle forceps deliberately applied

to the substantial face-up stuck head,
suctioned, washed, weighed and handed to us
by our teacher, sensitive to not intrude.

Scores good as I remember—
he became a bit jaundiced later—
as we learned what to do

and every little or big thing changed.
To nourish and wash and cuddle,
to coo and watch over in awe,

to be stretched beyond reasonable limits,
to show him off, to become the parents
we always wanted...or near enough.

8/1/13

Moving Closer
Arthur Ashe quoted again on Facebook

Long journey
every day one step or ten
but at least one

stepping into the unknown
every day show up
and walk as best you can.

"Start where you are"
one step from there
not knowing all the answers.

"Use what you have"
not wait until you have more...
money or friends or confidence or sleep.

"Do what you can"
always something
to move in a direction

you do not see from here
barely a wisp of an idea out there.
Trusting, patient, one step

is not too much to ask.
Show up not numb, not asleep
see what comes, what direction

the wind blows
when you raise a damp finger,
the goals unknown

only possibilities drawing you on.
With one choice then another
you move closer.

8/11/13

Shooting Stars

Lying back on the dew-damp
cedar-plank picnic table
in the backyard in Harper Woods
probably sometime in the late sixties.

Summer. Night. Crickets.
Looking for shooting stars with Dad.
Don't remember if we saw any,
but still the smell and feel of wet wood,
exhilaration of adventure out in the dark.

Probably the Perseid meteor shower
in August I'd guess, like now. Cool last night.
Out for an hour and a half after midnight:
Saw 3. No mosquitoes. Clear skies a while,
too much light. Tonight, warmer, mostly cloudy.
Five minutes: 1 mosquito. 0 shooting stars.

Watch clouds move, head tilted back on
wrought iron chair, neck propped by hood rolled down,
stars pop in and out of transient gaps.
Thinking back, like details of a movie playing,
remembering, connected to her back then,
connected to them.

In a few years I will leave home
with whatever I've learned about anything,
seeking expansion, liberation, to find who I am
in the age of upheaval, Vietnam War, assassination.
Rare would be these quiet moments of sharing again.

Young lack of understanding
how short number the days
how finite the opportunities

for the small things to build memories.
Do not know even now what turns out

to be important, what will stick to you like Velcro.

8/18/13

Good Books

I can't be trusted
with good book in hand,
for a while it becomes
more real than any reality.
And I am compelled
to turn pages long into the night
to find out what happens next...
and next...and next...

until some kind of
unexpected satisfying end
or maybe re-reading
certain favorite scenes
until I resolve again
to be more disciplined
and sleep. Stop pre-exhaustion
and be less greedy.

8/26/13

Sarah Horn Sings with Kristin Chenoweth
Before 10,000 people at the Hollywood Bowl

When stars align
and impossible piles on
impossible and then
you are called,

and when you are ready,
if you are brave enough and trust,
you say yes
and step up even

if heart is pounding
and knees give way
a little. You say yes
because you are in

the right place and time
to speak, to sing
for everyone. And
everyone's heart opens some.

You are seen
and heard and known
and for that bit at least
you are aligned with the stars

and life shifts,
not just for you,
but all around

and that is the gift.
What you do with what has been given,
what you do with the possibility of new direction,

what you say to the clamoring,
holding what you love close and releasing,
how you thrive without armor...and sing,

remembering who you are,
that is up to you, dear one
now and evermore.

8/28/13

Eric Whitacre: *Godzilla Eats Las Vegas*
With Elvises

There is music
takes itself so serious
and then

there is music
without a serious bone
that can sink in

to the dark places
and lighten
lift out of

and up
soaring without risk
of falling back.

8/28/13

Fearless in the Face of Panic
After Louise Penny at Cook Memorial Library

Not reasonable,
the root of the panic-weed cannot
be yanked out by reason.

Lives in the dungeon where
no one wants to go,
so dark, dank and ancient,
as if grown into the walls.

Where to find solace
if not in the rational
the factual, the simple plain real?

Dive into the depths then
unafraid of anything,
even if you can't swim
dive and return again,

cleansed.

9/8/13

Glass Blowing

From molten heat—
hotter than imaginable,
would vaporize flesh from bone—

the grains of fine sand
meld into the pre-thing
a flowing malleable blob

that could become anything.
Care, expertise, experience
patience, intuition, imagination

persistence, endurance, willingness
to withstand the heat
to create.

The drive once set in motion
sustains on some days, determination,
commitment and grit carries the others.

Once made, to risk rejection,
what if no one wants
this newborn creation?

Also to soak in praise,
amazement, be willing to share
what seems like magic.

9/9/13

Sitting for a Portrait
Emmett Johns

Sitting for a portrait
allowing yourself to be seen,
risking your own displeasure...
suspended...

Not like looking in a mirror—
backward exact duplication—
but filtered through
the eye, skill, fingers, kindness

of the artist,
trusting.

Not meant to be
an instant snapshot,
but catching through
color, shape and shadow

something of the hidden heart,
biography and essence.
And then...recognition...
and acceptance.

9/15/13

Few Days Ago

I said firmly to the spider
small fat and black,
"no jumping" and he jumped
not hearing or not believing
and landed on my shoe
and I stomped hard and he
vanished, neither on nor under.

9/16/13

Vacation

Unthinkable
in the old days
to be by water
and not go in.

Be by water
and not go in
early and often
dive in the waves
until fingers pruned

and Mom called us
from the far beach sand.
And we would
pretend not to hear
to get a few more
minutes of water.

Now 50 years later
to be by the lake
and look but not dip
watch boats sail
but no sand between the toes.
Not once in a week
feel waves lap at bare feet

walk along water's edge
listening.

9/28/13

4 AM

The Belt of Orion plain
between two branches of white pine
now at 4 AM.

Day is done, day begun
half moon has set
soon appears the sun

dissolved in drops of rain.

9/28/13

Mom's Birthday

When the worst has happened
and you lay flattened
like coyote on a mission

and no pump appears
to fill you with air,
no magical two-dimensional

resolution.
You pick yourself up
as best you can

breathe each breath
one by one
find someone to hold your hand

now and then.
Add one day to the next
until a string is strung with pearls.

Hold on until light
overtakes dark in the tunnel
and you are leaden no longer.

Not that grief is over or numbness
but fear is past and you accept
the worst has already happened.

You are still here
and might as well consider…
happiness.

10/6/13

After Talking with Dorothy

What did I think
of the new pain in her bones?
As if I could interpret

or predict the future
aside from any fear
and I considered and said

I don't know.
If cancer is worse…
healing is possible.

If you are off balance
and chronically stressed
balance can be restored.

If your reserves are empty
energy drained by grief
or small daily leaks

they can be refilled.
Get energy work, Reiki or other.
Do what gives you energy

laugh at a funny movie—
elicit all those good internal drugs.
You are doing very well.

In the face of great challenge
you have shown great strength
superwoman determination.

Will it be enough?
you didn't ask.
I don't know, I would have answered.

But I do know the good works
you continue to do.
I do know I will always love you.

So much is not in our control
that is the hard news,
that is the good news.

Show up fully present
every day do our best
and then leave the rest.

Whatever comes, however long
I am here, dear one
always and ever.

10/8/13

One Moment, Then the Next

Datura trumpets upward
ruffled edge filled to brim with sun.

Tiny "black and whites" flit in a white pine
searching for "crumbs" or cones.

Mailman delivers from his truck
clocks tick, sky clear cerulean.

Wind still for now
fly bumps against the glass.

The globe keeps turning as it does
wind kicks up from the far-off storm.

10/17/13

The Path

I am not an antidote to pain,
I don't even know
the surest way home,

but I have loved and lived some
and learned what works for me as I go,
making mistakes

falling off the cliff sometimes
dirt and gravel embedding in sensitive skin
and I can say this:

There is a light to follow,
there is a path laid out
as you go,

not one path for all or for all time,
but this moment
if you are patient,

if you trust kindness
and look past the rest,
there is a path to...something...

worth the wait.

10/21/13

Resilience

Of course I want to help
alleviate frustration,
not take in
what isn't even mine.

But how will you learn
your own resilience
if not by misjudging cliff's edge
and tumbling down,

grit and dirt scraping
into knees and palms.
Brushing off, deep breath,
maybe a good cry
of hopelessness, even temporary.

Then the climb up,
the resolve and stubbornness,
willingness to risk everything
at least once more.

10/22/13

Helicopter

A helicopter flew by my window,
no, not that kind,
the whirligig seeds from maple trees.

We don't have maple trees
only ash and oak, river birch and crab apple,
white pine and blue spruce,

so the seed had flown some distance

from the mother tree to
possibly bury itself here or be eaten.
Never know, but in the spring

after full germination
the green shoot might poke up
through newly thawed soil,

looking like a weed in my garden
and be pulled...
or the wind today might loft it

further to the forest or field
where it might become food
or future shade.

10/23/13

For Kelly's Mom

Control is an illusion
over children, not just
discipline when they are young,

but as years go on
what they pick up or put down
what choices they make,

what chances they take
oblivious to consequence
or a mother's heartbreak.

10/24/13

Emotional Stew
From talking with Crystal

Chunks of partly cooked carrots
and cubes of beef floating
on a low simmer.

No, not so specific as that,
some raw bits carefully minced,
some slowly softening in the heat,

all melding and marinating
in the broth of the others.
The aroma rises welcome

in the fall air, nourishing
in anticipation. This is not
about eating, but feeling,

how grief partially processed
has its chunks and raw places
and time has only healed so much,

not more. And the stew
continues to simmer on the burner,
even untended. Sometimes

someone may reach in for a sample
and declare it done, but nothing
is finished about grieving.

It is true light comes back
and the time in dark is shorter
and life returns, altered to be lived.

In the best case scenario
senses are sharpened,
gratitude enhanced,

life again vibrant in the moment.
In the worst case, life is always dark,
all colors grayed at least a bit,

the juice pre-sucked out of each day.
Like stew bubbling, the rich aroma
is only the precursor to consuming.

Choices are made about where and when,
with what dispatch or ceremony
we take to heart the nutrition.

10/25/13

Considering Mortality and Beyond
For my youngest sister, Dorothy

Your illness is
an open wound
for both of us.

Maybe a tendency to say:
Be done with it
and move on, blessing.

End the pain, bypass
future inevitable suffering,
the torment of the moment.

But we can do better than that.
We can forget a trajectory
where you go off alone

that doesn't include you and me—
of course wherever you are going next
the golden cord connects us.

If your days here
dwindle to nothingness
and I am left bereft,

where you are going next
the golden cord connects us.
If as it turns out

you stay here for a viable future arc,
well, me too. Here we are.

10/25/13

Walking Series

Fox colored cat
in bushes and out
seen by my door
would kill if she could
now into the wood

***

Five ducks in a pond
tails high inclined
searching the ground
under water not air

concentric circles
from each stroke
radiate out and out
each shimmer-ripple

catching the slanted light

10/27/13

To Lift Sorrow Out

To lift sorrow out of the heart
to lay the burden down
to turn that weight of stone
over to giant ethereal hands,

what would it be like
to be so light?

Heart beats without restraint
joy floods the interstitial spaces,
at least a chance of hopefulness
as each beat floods the body with love

and cells with lovely oxygen.

10/31/13

Preparing for Echocardiogram
Experiment in releasing anxiety

Like silk scarves pulled
out of a magician's top hat
so streams anxiety out
of my healing heart

colorful connected squares
then a dark stretch, then color
flowing, impossibly flowing
more and more than

could be lodged in there
until it is done,
the last flowing out
with a final flourish.

And the heart is storing nothing,
beating strong, steady, calm,
enriched blood carrying oxygen.
Breathe out, breathe in...

and on and on and on...

11/1/13

Towards the End

Who knows if
towards the end she
mostly lived vicariously

and that was enough
until the cocooning
to be who she was becoming.

Or if her days seemed full
with the myriad minutiae
vitally important to her

or what used to be
distant memories
that seemed quite real

and that was enough
to get through one day
and another, until...

11/2/13

Changes Everything

It is possible
to forget good exists...

and niceness
or to discount their existence

as if life is a video game
full of unwarranted violence,

inevitable, not even remarkable
anymore, but then remembering

at some point starving for
a little kindness

and receiving without
thought of return

as if we all were neighbors
sometimes in need of a cup of sugar

and that momentary easy connection
changes everything...

back.

11/4/13

Dreaming of Dance

In second grade because I asked
my mother signed me up for dance class,

not ballet as I wanted, but tap
at my old school I had not been sorry to leave.

Taught by two teen girls to a class of gazelles
with me the lone elephant, not that I was fat,

but taller and bigger than any other.
I had just gotten my first grownup strapless

Sunday-best church shoes and now the shoemaker
had to add straps, with taps that tapped

when I walked up the aisle in church
and showed shiny when I knelt for Communion.

I practiced diligently in our cement basement,
tap step, tap step, 1, 2, 3, 4. Shuffle ball change….

But in class I became the oaf, chastised with:
"Why didn't you practice?"

The recital came with a beatnik costume requirement:
a man's white long-sleeved dress shirt and black tights.

I didn't have these things, nor the money to buy them
and my Mom complained I think. In any case

I wore my pastel pink Easter dress,
lipstick applied at school before our performance.

After we danced, applause led to an encore.
What a glow! No photo though.

***

As a teen I tried to teach myself
from a tiny picture book of ballet positions,
my "barre" a half-wall by the hall stairs
as I pretended to be graceful.

***

A second chance at dance after college,
Ann Arbor *Adult Beginning Ballet*, strict dress code:

black long-sleeved leotard, pink tights and shoes. Again a giant among sylphs, the only one who had never previously "taken."

When first learning *grand jeté*, both my feet were air-born
and instead of a verbal pat: " Keep your arms in first, Marge…"

(not my actual name). Still it was flying.
With a back strain halfway through and a move out of state

my "career" was finished, though I still keep those shoes.

11/5/13

The Joke

A dream in which
my (now dead) mother
her face rather angular and gaunt,

said, "I could really use a joke."
I am not good at remembering jokes,
the set up, the timing, the punch line,

but I came up with one I recently read
about the woman, arsenic, and the pharmacist
and woke telling it from the mist.

11/6/13

After Roberta Who Asked

What is grief
if not indispensible,
the dark murk in which
light can be...light.

Perception askew
I ask you
what is life without loss,
without loving so much

leaving makes a difference.
And yet, and yet
it cannot be the end of it.
An end and a beginning

as it always was,
as it always will be
not just for me.

2013, Surgery
Healing through Re-Writing the Old Story

11/9/13

ER 2AM
Condell Hospital

How soon to get help,
to say out loud I am bleeding,
how long to wait, how much blood

to lose before the inevitable.
To be smart this time, transparent,
to not pretend even to myself

to be superwoman, able to handle anything.
Even if this happened before
to the old me who would not risk telling.

When to wake my husband?
(These things often happen at night.)
Or fear peaks in the dark...or

pain of one kind or another is heightened.
To not be embarrassed or shamed
by the body bleeding

while I was not looking,
one moment OK, the next
gushing bright red between the legs,

not labor and delivery this time.
No one knows, truly knows why.
Tests have been done

and reassurances given. Yet with little warning,
one moment out to dinner, driving home,
sitting in the rocker and then standing up

and the liquid-warm rush, the dash
and the toilet bowl bright red plus clots.
How much can safely be lost

before losing consciousness?
Let us not test that hypothesis this time,
but make an effort to stay calm.

Massage the acupressure point at big toenail's
bottom outer edge, one foot then the other.
Take *Sabina*, which usually does the trick

but...not this time. Repeat and repeat.
How long to work at it and wait?
Now...we go now,

overcome any reluctance,
use that precious insurance,
trust help in the form of tests,

people waiting on the night shift
for you (or someone) to come...
and you come.

11/12/13

Little Sister

She seemed so fiercely certain
my heart was strong
she pulled me along a bit
into that sureness of belief

which wove into my speech
as emotional calisthenics.
Strong, steady, calm heart,
affirming in whichever order,

directions from me to the body,
spoken aloud for clarity:
This is what I want of you,
not shying away from reality.

In that familiar place immersed
in the sea of pure possibility,
where the worlds that might be,
or might have been, meld together

in that expansive room. To be clear:
This is the life I am co-creating
setting out the pattern plain, the map
to follow...simple and practical.

11/13/13

Cockeyed

Bracing for a blow
in case there is a blow

a hit upside the head
with a railroad tie

and all the known up to then...
cockeyed.

And all from now on...
unrecognizable.

11/13/13

Observing Geese

Herd of geese grazing
on the sun-strewn field

not flying in, to or on
in elegant ephemeral formation,

but webbed feet walking over grass
beaks down to now cold ground,

solitary as if what previously
held them together,

what instinct, what telepathy,
what biology or evolutionary alignment

was silenced
temporarily

and it was each for themselves
until...necessity.

11/14/13

Awareness

I am not stupid.
I know what is going on,
no use trying to cram it
to a remote corner of my mind,

not healthy even as
short-term survival strategy.
Reasonable fear has overtaken me.
I know I have skills

and I now call on them.
What was nothing again
has become everything,
filled all the space there is

to overflowing.
I am brave as before,
I hang on, not tumbling over
the customary cliff.

But I am bone-tired,
though still trusting-patient.
I am weary of this
and long to choose happiness.

11/17/13

From Inside

Low, sustained belly-growl of thunder,
glass lashed by ice pellets
needles clumped frozen on white pine,
flexible branches frantically bowing and scraping.
The raw beginning, the whimper end.
Sometimes want to talk about it,
sometimes anything else but.

11/18/13

Uterus 1

What is a uterus?
I know what you think,
what a question for
a grown woman to ask.

What is a uterus and
what is lost when one is lost?
Not just a bit of pear-shaped
tissue smaller than my fist,

part of a girl from the first,
small enough to fit tucked inside
with the rest and big enough to hold a baby,
strong enough to deliver one and

flexible enough to shrink back down.
Every month after a time, preparation…
until such time as moon-phase ends…
the possibilities both less and more.

A uterus as physical fact,
as psychological symbol, emotional cords
of life playing out over and over:
Get ready, slough off, get ready…

until enough.

11/18/13

New Doctors
AP and VT

It is possible that
through your trained fingers,
education, heart and intuition

I will reshape my body
to what is now imagined
and what *was* melds into

the new what *is*.
Trusting this is not
yet another choice with
unintended harsh consequences,

but a release from
a prison of a sort with
concomitant healing.

Trusting my training
is not wishful thinking,
but real tested skills

to shape from provided clay,
and drawn into the guided space,
to show up...and become

more and more who I came for.

Though I longed to heal
as my strong independent self—
high vibration energy sculpting matter,

releasing the wounded past,
returning back to me what was lost—
this is the means that showed up.

My innate gift,
should I choose to accept this,
is to recognize and say: "Yes."

My job is to be myself,
not eliminating any errant parts,
using my intuition, my X-ray vision,

my trust fulfilling expectation.

11/19/13

To Trust Again?

Today I am trying hard
to believe in better

but like a woman with
a recklessly unfaithful lover

a decision had to be made
to draw the line...and now

to be asked to trust...again...
I am trying hard to believe.

11/19/13

Another New Surgeon

How would you *feel*
if someone you just met
was going to make decisions

affecting the quality
(and quantity) of every day
for the rest of your life?

Let us say this trust—
for it is extreme trust that is asked—
had previously been misplaced,

promises made and not kept
with hard direct consequences,
could you now say yes?

Not how would you *think*
reason, rationalize,
but in your heart, your gut,

deep in the marrow of your bones
could you find forgiveness
(for yourself included)

and forget the checkered past,
stepping forward into what could be
(*if only*) a bright long future

of sweet promise fulfilled?

11/20/13

To Tell You

I wish I could tell you
I planned it all out—
intelligent, educated, insightful as I am—

but no I did not,
as much as I healed...
like bailing a leaky rowboat.

And instead of sinking
I swam in the river
or floated or someone came

to carry me the next bit,
not to the end of it
but enough.

11/21/13

Safe and Spooned

I am safe
lying here spooned
with my sleeping husband

who is warm
and smells slightly of cloves.
We are softly breathing

and music is playing.
Lying here under a thick duvet
it is a warm cocoon.

I am safe
pain-free
breathing easily

heart beats regularly.
When I rise
I slip back into the room

and walk effortlessly
out the door
down the hall into

my own silence.

11/23/13

Kinds of Anxiety

There is a kind of anxiety
that comes from the unknown
and a kind of anxiety
that comes from the past,
fear of repeat...or worse.

Anxiety that comes from
knowing too well what can happen—
the statistics—forgetting
they do not apply to individual acts.

Anxiety transferred osmotically from someone,
from feeling particularly unlucky
or disconnected or alone.
Anxiety as a reasonable response
though not helpful and hard on the heart.

Roll all kinds into a firm ball
like thick mud or cookie dough
and with a windup to prepare
and a step in proper form
(or just the desire to release)

throw so far no one will ever
exceed the distance,
so far anxiety will never
come oozing or drizzling
or whizzing back.

11/23/13

Uterus 2

This pear-shaped organ
there from my beginning,
part of being a woman

that grew my babies
from implant to watermelon
and rhythmically delivered them.

This uterus almost all
that is left of that time in my life,
but not quite, not what makes me...me.

What a ride we had,
the early irregularity,
the scares in the middle,

then settling down and
two hard pregnancies,
two hard deliveries then

two independent unique babies
that likely left some cells
lodged in my body researchers now say.

The aches, the bloating, the blood,
the cycling with the moon,
then stop, then start, repeat and repeat.

Now this for the sweet uterus:
Excision, examination, revelation,
loss of connection,

cells taken by decision
necessary as far as can be known.
Reasonable even...

throat tightens with emotion.
"All of me, why not take all of me?"
as the song goes,

but I am lucky to have left
so much more.
OK, then....

11/27/13

Rewind: Senseless Tragedy
Victor

*"Whatever you're meant to do, do it now.
The conditions are always impossible."*
Doris Lessing (1919-2013)

From the moment of impact
of tons of train with ordinary sedan,
metal wheels on metal track,

100 yards to stop....
Rewind, go back
to leaving home, maybe distracted or

hurrying, thinking of something else, not paying attention.
Heading east on Old Mill Road,
gates go down. Other cars around.

Early on a Saturday afternoon,
the week before Hanukkah, day one,
falls on a late Thanksgiving.

Before that, getting the job,
all the surgeries, moving.
Fellowship, residency, internship

medical school, college,
all the every-days that fill a life unfolding,
headed for somewhere.

Skills learned and honed,
shaped by everything into the person he became.
Before that, high school, achievement,

goals to focus on, a future laid out before him.
And grade school, kindergarten,
back to being born as his mother's son.

What to make of a short life
front to back, back to front,
a split second thoughtless decision

undoing all the previous choices,
all the hopes and nurturing,
persistence and determination.

The impact radiates out into space-time:
to the train engineer and witnesses,
emergency response workers,

to the colleagues, friends, family,
all who knew or cared,
all who almost met,

what might have been now denied.
How to soak it all in,
not forever remaining numb,

let anger and sorrow and disbelief,
disappointment and loss and grief
mix with acceptance and gratitude

for the days there were,
all of it to be felt until he
melts into the past,

no longer spoken of in present tense.
Mourned and remembered as if
one life is all we have.

Now death divides us,
one side of the veil from the other,
but there he is still and we are here

with something, some purpose
to accomplish. If we are still breathing,
heart still beating...beating...
beating...

surely for some reason.

12/1/13

Shadow and Sun

Yesterday at midday the stately trees lining the drive

laid out their skeletons long on the ground

Today those slanted shadows are gone

a blanket covering the sun

12/4/13

Still Thinking of Victor

Who among us
has not been careless
for a moment
more than once

and each time
escaped unscathed,
each time "lucky?"
I guess.

Did you learn
from the close call,
heart pounding
with surge of adrenaline

at what might have been,
to be vigilant and always careful?
Or in the course of days
did you get swept along

by the next thing
and being human
imperfection, push the limit
of distraction,

forget to plant feet on the ground,
forget to breathe
noticing what is around you,
requiring another rescue?

And sometimes for reasons
better left undisclosed…
the cosmic mystery of it…
time is up.

12/6/13

Faith

In the darkness

knowing

not alone exactly

aware of the Singularity

unsure of the path

stepping forward anyway

12/8/13

White Woman from Illinois on Mandela
Posted by John Flynn on *Facebook*

"I am not a saint, unless you think of a saint as a sinner who keeps on trying."
Nelson Mandela (1918-2013)

He might be the first to say
he was ordinary,
a man making choices with great clarity,

understanding consequences
to holding hate and anger close,
how one gets burned
and nothing is accomplished.

To say now he was awe-inspiring,
to raise him so high in sainthood,
select media-glorifying snippets to focus on,
reducing him to an icon on a pedestal

does him and us a disservice
for it assumes *we* cannot also *be* better,
do better, make the forgiving choices.
It assumes he was a hero above us, beyond us,

a mythological figure, not flesh and bone.
It says we admire from afar but do not aspire
to be something held so high...
and that is wrong.

We are all capable of better,
more conscious loving acts.
We are all awesome healers
no matter our circumstance.

We do not have to reflexively perpetuate
old patterns that do not serve us.
We can heal within and radiate healing out.

Start now, start somewhere,
some small breach, maybe love yourself
a little or a little more today
as a way of remembering him,
honoring a long life of sacrifice
and ultimate joy—as a choice.

12/10/13

Dear Uterus:

Despite the many challenges
you have done all that was asked,
bore two healthy babies
expanded with their growth,
and expelled them as gently as can be.

The monthly cycles varied late and early
too much blood or too little,
exposure to all manner of common chemicals
phytoestrogens, plastics, airborne particles,
still cycling, cycling

long after eggs were gone
and most women done
cycling with the moon.
Here we are again
and loss is imminent
no other options I can see

and I have looked and worked
and healed and asked to be revealed
the answer to the biopsy results,
to the bleeding, the fearful surprises.
This is the answer:
to go where I am sent,

to follow the path laid out,
to feel the loss,
to honor the service
and release.
To be myself, as innately curious,
eager to connect and learn as always.
As willing to share and listen and live...
as always. Amen.

And now to fill the closed fist
of a 61 year-old uterus
with love and more love,
to let love wash out
anything unserving
or lower in energetic vibration.
Let love radiate out and out
and heal and trust all will be well.

And all will be well.

12/10/13

Back to a Single Surgery
After talking with surgeons, SG and AP

A 10 centimeter cut he said,
at the pubic hair line he said,
avoiding the compromised abdomen mostly,
allowing for the very small possibility
of any necessity for further surgery,

depending on word back from the lab.
If this is not the *au courant*
popular high-tech strategy
using robots or laparoscopy,
it is right for me.

My job is to recognize when
the heart and mind as one
have spoken.
I am a healer
and this is the form.

12/16/13

Addendum to the Life List
Hysterectomy

Two new scars mostly hidden,
6 ½ in. and 2 in. by sight,
held together by stitches and glue,
intuition after the exploration.

Pain at this point, yes,
but less than you might imagine.
To stretch, to roll, to sleep on the side,
to get up and walk almost normally,

to be myself sometimes,
almost vibrant and then
the feeling of turning gray.
Pay attention! Get back to bed in time,

do not fall or forget to be aware
of the usually small things,
one step then another, one step then another,
a breath, a beat...breath, beat...,

making the way upstairs,
snow falling softly,
at dusk of the third day.

12/18/13

Post-Surgery

New born
back out of the womb
with uterus gone,
ultrasensitive
to every light, movement, sound.

Cannot walk much,
cannot talk as if
had grown to adult,
but re-born to a world
of altered possibility,

not as you might say:
restricted. But free, free
from previous limitation,
all doors may now open,
she may now choose

to step through.

12/19/13

Thrown Again into the Frazzle Machine
Phone call from Dr. Alok Pant

How long does it take to
find the ground

to wrap the mind around
another cancer diagnosis

life ongoing
remember that

the choice made
one recent night

to live...still
much to do

who am I now
alone and in relation to.

12/20/13

A Tiny Bit

By definition
no fun to be
a curmudgeon

why bother
with the smile
upside down

12/20/13

Dodged a Bullet

Dodged a bullet
indeedy,

missed not by much
what might have been,

a path not easily taken,
but for sure

a woman awakened
yet again.

At first a new-born
at first a bit stunned

every sensory receptor
for light, smell, taste, sound

SO LOUD
almost unbearable,

yet how alive, how beautiful!
In that night a choice made,

in those heart-pounding hours
a risk taken trusting,

and surrender,
not a promise exactly,

but a divine pact:
If still here in the morning

it must be for some reason...
go to it.

12/20/13

Partnership
Of Alok and Melissa Pant

I wanted to tell you about partnership,
not mine but observed,

a surgeon and anesthesiologist
like a pitcher and catcher on a

championship team, in sync late in the season,
bringing out the best in each other,

not having to speak
to get the good result.

Though I do not know them yet
I can see and know the effect

of their willingness to listen,
to be flexible without rigid preconception,

trusting me as I trust them,
as I put my future in their capable hands.

As it happens, they are husband and wife,
partners declared in the rest of their life.

It made a difference I tell you,
it made a difference to me.

Not set up this way,
I wanted, but did not control

and as things unfolded
I let go,

I listened and
let go.

Let the outcome be
better than I could ever orchestrate,

better than I could ever imagine.
Got out of the way,

chose...yes,
to let it happen,

somehow...through life's messiness
and mystery, to land in the right place.

12/21/13

Accomplishment

Pure drops on glass
prisms for the colored lights
the freeze is coming they say
but for now it is rain
not slick though shiny driveway
and I went out with you
as we used to.

12/22/13

All Is Well

No sun
but snow reflection
each still branch coated
but not burdened.
The ice coming they say
but not yet today.
All is well
all is well.

12/23/13

Mother
In the long night

I missed my mother
and wanted to call her
when my life was sinking
into the deep end.

But she was gone
long before she was gone,
her self peering out
only occasionally.

I felt her there
in some way with the rest,
no way she would ever miss this,
being at the hospital, her realm.

Not that she spoke to me,
not that I felt her touch,
but somehow her energy…
that must be it…that wisp I felt.

Now looking at the plant she sent
after some other surgery,
some past health calamity,
a mixed planting that was

pierced with fuzzy pussy willow stalks
in perfect harmony once,
but five years later was scraggly
some plants dead, some brown, no flowers.

Though not as esthetically
beautifully balanced as before,
though I remember to water only
intermittently, it sits in the sun,

varied shapes and shades of green,
and grows some and reminds me.

12/25/13

Cervix

The cervix she
is hidden sweet
in the dark and depths,
bending and nodding to caress
the lover's presence,
opening her lips to the dew
that might become
someone new.

Now the cervix
from her waiting stance is taken
to be tested
with the rest that is shaken free,
leaving what is fine and true
to continue.

A loss not obvious,
not seeming to have a voice
separate from the uterus,
but worthy of her own
consideration,
also there from the beginning,

the door that monthly opened
now a corridor blunt-ended.

12/27/13

Effects of Anesthesia

Struggle with words in a line
whether thought, written, said or read,

the worst of the fog
induced by the decision,

the necessity pressed upon me
for surgery...

and the attendant anesthesia
I would have done without,

but instead lobbied for the minimum.
And found, or were sent, two partners

willing to let go the usual sacrosanct
way of treating everyone as average

according to one standard of care,
who listened and were flexible, willing to be

creative, intelligent and compassionate.
The practical result was worth it.

Though not all side-effects were eliminated,
the most egregious were much lessened.

Still left with the body detoxing a bit,
the mind foggy a bit,

less than last time...
and not as long.

The heart managed to keep on
and the organ systems resumed

and restoring sleep eventually came to me,
true deep sleep, not drug-induced mini-coma.

And most practically, the speed of healing,
the brilliant reduction of pain,

the quick coming back to myself
from those dark temporary depths,

the sheer cliff that one night
when I was lost and desperate to get home.

12/28/13

From the Perspective of the Tree
Death of Paul Walker

A tree can kill
someone in a car
a friend is driving 100 miles per hour
who loses control
for reasons unknown,

a red Ferrari, say,
that hits a pole
that used to be a tree
or hits the tree

according to the laws of physics
and bursts into flame
and no one asks
what happened to the tree

absorbing the impact
scorched by the fire.
An innocent tree by all accounts
did not jump in front of

or behave recklessly
but raised its leaves each spring
and spread out its shade
quietly beholden to no one.

12/28/13

Home from the Hospital
Remembering

On the second or third night
I woke to check the clock alarm
to find it dark and thinking I had
inadvertently in my fog pressed a button
I turned the light switch
to find it still dark and noticed
the cold and all around quiet and dark
and went to the window...dark
but for a truck down the road
with yellow flashing lights.

So I knew they knew
and did not need me to call
or wake my husband
as it grew colder.
And I knew I couldn't go anywhere
but the nest in my bed
to wait as warm as I could
for the power to go back on
which in time it did.

12/30/13

Loss

What once led to the chamber
of possible new life
is now a dead-end corridor

that is to say
not a welcoming door
to internal expansiveness

nobody but me
will miss.
Even I may not

notice.

12/30/13

Energy Restored

What is it like to not be
hyper-vigilant to bleeding,
not just on a cycle, somewhat expected

though with ovaries gone,
still sometimes mostly
an inconvenient saturation,

but to wake from a dream sticky wet,
feel the ache, the bloat as if,
and then the gush, the clots,

the hanging on as if young?
To not be tied to that
worrying about *that*,

always prepared just in case,
tampons and *Sabina* in my pockets,
every night pressing the acupressure points

for bleeding to forestall any.
Always alert as a default.
What energy it took,

hopeful it would run its course
and stop, until the crisis
and the surgical choices.

Testing upon testing over years,
and all that time the energy depleted,
being prepared, always prepared.

Dashing off at a restaurant.
Wondering while driving, sleeping,
walking, sitting, talking, working,

stretching, biking, anything.
For years and now...
the quiet loveliness...of nothing.

The flow of energy diverted back to...
anything...everything waiting.

2014, Post-Surgery Life Resuming

1/2/14

Another Serious Diagnosis

There is a part
that says why me

and there is a part
even from the beginning

that suspects or sees
opportunity

1/3/14

First Night

In the dark hours
of the first night after

it would not seem possible—
laughter—

not at first or easily
but it always comes back to this

sometimes being silly
being light enough

to break out, let out
rise above and…

love.

1/6/14

May Be Called New Year

At some point
not predetermined
after the parents are gone
there comes a certain freedom,

birthing yourself this time
without constraint of approval
or even unconscious disapproval.
To take the step

that had been invisible,
whatever had gone before
wiped clean and now
without thinking too much,

without necessarily having a plan,
put fear aside replaced by love
healed by love, and
loving yourself as the seed of everything

be the crystal that forms.

1/14/14

Door Into

Cancer as the door
not obvious into...something
and out of what had been,

a sign that time is over.
If the door is chosen
and opens what then?

Exploration
choices, changes, chances.
What had been

now seen with less distortion
in rarified light sometimes
and inevitable insights.

Not the culmination perhaps
not the darkest thing that can happen
just cause and effect,

just a simple door that opens: *If*...
which leads to...*Life*
and possible awareness of happiness.

1/15/14

History of the Hernia
Umbilical then incisional

At first it was small,
the diameter of a little fingertip
discovered during a routine checkup,
another brick added to the already
unbearably heavy load and I went
out to my car after and sobbed.

For a while nothing was done,
avoid coughing while lying down.
A decision made to go
back to my old surgeon,
who (as it turned out) did not remember
singing with me before surgery nor
the poem I wrote for him, did not remember *me*.

That's OK, so many surgeries in ten years since
all that water under the bridge for him…. Still.
Potential surgery led to the EKG,
which led to the stress test
and all the rest of the hullabaloo.
Panic ensued (heart). Surgery off track
though I was fit.

Waiting…
while the dust settled, tests done, decisions made,
how to be myself in midst of all this.
The hernia, still a small thing,
pushed to the side while I was a square peg
trying to fit into a round hole,
falling deeper into the bottomless medical pit.
And yet…

Eventually the hernia grew large enough
to insist and cancer also came to visit
and verified mutation. Unexpected help
on the healing path from my past and
the hernia (almost an afterthought)
got rolled into all that. Two new surgeons.

One surgeon had to leave on New Year's Eve
and likely lack of communication with the new one
led to the first mistake as an incision was stitched
and re-opened and re-stitched and the surrounding tissue
pulled like delicate fabric almost rotting.

Over time, after initial recovery,
the new incision led to a new hole which was patched,
only local anesthesia at my request.
For whatever combination of reasons:
too small mesh, inauspicious environment, error,
my fall on the escalator at Newark airport,
the morning cough, BMI, planets not favorably aligned…
the fix did not hold forever or even very long.

Another new hole.
Despite the determined struggle to heal
which worked for a while—
with help and trust and patience—
the hole grew enough for insides to push through
and threaten life if guts could not be shoved back in,
daily both painful and dangerous.

Once more into the fray, dear one,
another experienced recommended surgeon.
The hernia the prime focus now.
Let's be honest, here at least,
I felt a failure for not healing from this,
all the past life revelations,
all the energy healing sessions
and previous healing successes.
Here I was facing surgery again.

Precautions taken and preparation.
Energy healers at the surgery to act for me
and still...
extreme pain, ER, ileus, heart arrhythmia, seroma
no food, no sleep for days. Deal as best I can...
trusting, stuck with what *is*
in this inflexible paradigm.
More healing, more thrashing around.
Anxiety now a major player,
a frequent uninvited understandable companion.

Daily life going on,
losses and joys and keeping on
as best one can.
The hernia *per se* does not return,
the hole from inside to out.
But the body does not grow muscle into mesh
and skin hangs down unconnected
and abdomen looks 5 months pregnant at least.

Not painful mostly,
not threatening
though distressing
more than I can say.

Years...then another diagnosis
another likely abdominal surgery,
the stated possibility
of rolling it all into one ball.
But no...for good reasons...no.

Here we are,
the large oval composite mesh
all that is holding my front together,
abdominal muscles separated
to right and left.
Sometimes tummy flatter than other times,
never appearance of normal,

can't suck the gut in even,
skin flap hiding the new large incision.

Not wanting to borrow trouble
not ungrateful,
this is not painful—in the physical.
But this is not right
and the mind goes back to it
like the tongue to a jagged tooth.
Some days I feel sadness
overcome me, though not mostly.

Where does that leave us,
where does that leave us,
when all the past fish
are pulled out, examined and dried?
At the edge of a well-documented…
potential…totally remarkable…miracle.

1/15/14

Fact of the Matter

The word cancer
said with loose lips
as if extreme danger,

as if epitome of fear
not knowing the body
sweeps away these cells

ordinarily,
not knowing the body
could use a little help

to restore balance sometimes.
Jumping to conclusions
insufficiently warranted,

not the true fact of it.

1/15/14

Snow

The thing about snow
is its renewable nature
its innate ability to
soften, dampen and freshen
to cover dark or imperfection
to be molded around and by
to hold crystalline memory
to brighten even in
moonless, star-free dark

1/17/14

Changing Rules

I wish I could tell you
one more hopeful thing,
but you will go on remembering
things as they are.

I wish I could say to you
from certainty of the future,
but all I know is in the heart
I can feel the truth.

At some points, maybe begun already,
human paths will diverge.
Those tied to the past
will stay in this carved reality

and those untethered to what was
will not exactly drift into space,
but click onto another track
with more expansive possibility.

I see the vision already,
the rules of chemistry changing,
history re-written to include
stories that could have been told.

Everywhere mothers with small children
or a young butcher with a camera
creating or capturing beauty to share
or to keep somewhere.

I can see, and you
what there is to live for,
why being sensitive is not a curse
but a gift

and choices will be made
to use it.

1/17/14

Continual Conundrum

More words are
tumbling all over themselves
to line up with meaning,

to express something vast or minute,
tell a universal or unique story
maybe recognized by someone.

If I stop to rest
they persist or drift off,
a loss irredeemable.

If I do not rest
the battery depletes and words
cannot cut through the fog.

Balanced on a needle
with the angels dancing or still,
I try to do what I can.

1/18/14

Vanished

The mother bereft
of a disappeared girl
just when her guard was let down.

The girl, a woman emerging,
old enough to defend herself
and yet still gone.

Worse in some ways
than for-certain knowing,
the body seen through

red-rimmed eyes.
Still hope, though slim,
the beloved daughter might be found,

at least released from
one kind of hell
to know what happened.

1/19/14

Portrait of Michael Smith
Concert at Lake County Folk Club

He was not old
but old enough
to be comfortable

exposing bits of his humanness,
to be felt and heard and seen
without disguise sometimes, to be
clever and mischievous, gracious and generous.

To be naked enough
to make us cry or laugh,
you have to put in the years,
put in your time as apprentice,
to gather the stories, weave or live them,
to know what is what,
to see the risks and still be willing

enough so some pieces fit,
and brave enough or fearless
to *go* out and *let* out some
of the accumulated multitudes of children,
all the practice paying off, the determination
to deliver the songs yet again.
Amen.

1/21/14

Awareness of Progress

It is easy to mistake
steady progress for
standing still.

It is easy to forget
past accomplishments
always looking forward

mind racing ahead
with expectation

forgetting when a sound
night's sleep was a triumph
and a pain-free day unlikely

when bending to tie a shoe
or standing long enough to brush teeth
was in some ways a delight

when walking with a normal gait
was only a hopeful dream
now realized...again.

1/23/14

For Midge and Me
Thank you

Landing on the other side
of the chasm yawning dark,
not one spectacular risky leap
but a pontoon bridge held up
by willing hands of all stripes.
Step by step re-writing the old story
to heal and still remember,
to let go control and gain
more than the desired outcome.
I can see the patterns
but not explain
one day here, one day across again.

And now…what then?
The unexpected guarantee for
"better than I could possibly imagine."

1/25/14

Non-Surgical Solutions

If you go to a surgeon with a problem
he or she, according to arduous curriculum,
will likely give you a surgical solution.

Rare is it a surgeon might say:
Listen to more music to calm or exhilarate,
dance or paint, sing or write,
walk or sit in meditation to clear your mind

and find your answers. Or: You may be best served
by an energy healer or spiritual mentor to reconcile
and harmonize interior places that are out of balance.
A massage, a vacation, or being self-loving is just the ticket.

The surgeon, who is human,
will likely go with obvious strengths.
Remember if you can
the broader universe we live in,

not everything cut and dried and knowable,
remember the individual shades, tones, variations,
the sea of pure potentiality. Studies have been done that say

what the doctor believes in makes a difference to outcome,
remember....

1/27/14

Ready to Be Released Back into the Wild
Alok Pant, 6 week follow-up

Freed from captivity
no restrictions but
common sense.
Ease back into it,
pay attention.
Call if there are concerns.

If that inner voice says no,
but stubborn I ignore,
be aware
of dire consequence,
better to listen
with no expectation.

Let go and step out,
resume or rebuild or restore.
In this bitter cold
be grateful for warmth
for breath, for food, for resilience,
be glad of company on the journey.

Rejoice in the ability to see beauty,
to feel generous and strong,
to walk with ultimate purpose,
to sing the song I came to sing.

1/28/14

Six-Week Follow-Up

What happened yesterday when
all the anxiety I had unknowingly
kept barely at bay
came surging through the floodgates?

I was unprepared for
the elevation in blood pressure
the shallowness of breath
the confusion in the darkness.

Why should something so simple
in someone so apparently aware
wreak such havoc?
I like this doctor...a lot.

My experience with this has been
nothing short of a miraculous,
life-changing string of healing miracles.
Why then this trepidation?

Good question.
Not lack of skill, but history maybe
not lack of support, but fear perhaps
some new bad thing would jump out at me,

another unexpected unwelcome bogeyman
to shake my newfound foundation.
Or...nothing is wrong, all is healed beautifully
restrictions lifted, I am sent back

to regular life with all the usual expectations
and none of the old fitness and energy,
none of the necessary resilience.
Again awakened...now what?

Without the internal and external
prime focus on daily care
the old routine set aside mostly
(is this even true, I don't know)?

Like before, can I maintain insights,
can I remember who I am...now
when all around urges me to
step back and resume my old trajectory?

Where am I going anyway?
I thought I was better than this
had it all conquered, life figured out
knew what songs I came to sing.

Part of me is disappointed in me,
that familiar feeling of not being enough,
or not good enough. And I have to
emphatically say to myself:

Ridiculous!
Feet on the ground,
heart open, I remember:
Be kind. As I find my way, be kind.

1/28/14

On Imperfection
For Corax

On the other side of darkness
the past looks far away,
and if I didn't know better,
mostly forgotten.

Live in the now,
isn't that what they say?
I agree mostly and also intend
to remember my lessons:

not to repeat same old mistakes,
not to let the unconscious pilot the course,
to remember to breathe,
to always be kind and

to forgive, every day to forgive
imperfection. For here we learn
by being in form, subject to complex patterns
we cannot sense or anticipate.

If we were perfect—
which we are somewhere—
what would be the point of
choosing to go to Earth-school?

As long as we are here—
those numbered precious days,
those rare allotted minutes—
we have work to do.

Get on with it.

1/28/14

My Own Tribute
Pete Seeger 1919-2014

Although Pete Seeger
traveled here and there,
now he is everywhere.

Though there are those
who would make him saint (or sinner)
he doesn't care, if he ever did

for he knows best what we all know
how the days are numbered rare,
now Pete Seeger is everywhere.

Not up on a pedestal I'm sure he'd say,
he was an honest man with a mission,
not down in the gutter either, nor scared,
now Pete Seeger is everywhere.

Singing in his confident voice
inviting us to sing along,
songs that we all know and share,
now Pete Seeger is everywhere.

Not in charge of anything big,
working day to day for the voiceless ones,
a determined "ordinary" man who cared,
now Pete Seeger is everywhere.

All the stories of something kind he said,
from everyone who met him or wished they did,
but when Toshi died last year, he died a bit I swear,
now Pete Seeger is everywhere.

His energy released from form now joins us,
not buried in the ground nor ashes spread,
not in some fancy world "up there,"
now Pete Seeger is everywhere...

singing, playing, chopping wood,
encouraging, traveling, doing good,
planting seeds, making a better place,
playing banjo, eye to eye, face to face,
exhorting us to care, I swear

now Pete Seeger is everywhere.

1/28/14

Still Fragile

Released from the cage of frailty
no matter how technically voluntary
or apparently temporary.

Free now to rebuild or rediscover
strength. Use full breath to open…
to expand…to unlock.

Today is the day to try it
take a step out
one small step

and don't slip back.

1/29/14

Conscious

Almost too shallow
to qualify as breath
too little oxygen gettin' in
yet still indisputably conscious
as evidenced by…this

1/29/14

Reflection
*Post six-week follow-up
with (and for) Alok Pant*

Disappointed in myself
for not being more focused,
more linear with lists, less anxious,

as if anxiety would lessen
despite circumstance—and yet
at least for less time this time,

if increased intensity.
And maybe to consider
I did what was necessary exactly.

***

You are extraordinary,
still willing to be seen,
not flattened yet or made cautious

by life experience,
and may it ever be so.
Your kindness, interested voice, gentle touch,

engaged listening, personal warmth,
easy wide smile, intelligent curiosity.
What is it I like most about you?

Your energy, your welcoming,
your ability to see eye to eye
and willingness to be flexible

and reasonable, adding intuition to the mix,
backed by recent research and common sense:

First do no harm,
likely benefit exceeds expected risk.
And yet, I was still anxious.

Why?
Not just neural patterns now reinforced,
but reasonable fear

based on past experience
that however benign the countenance,
bad can come of this:

Bogeymen jump out of the closet leaving me
flattened, scared and scarred. All that came before
inaccessible and gone, a distant memory,

and all that comes later begins now.
Who am I in relation to this
looming theoretical dark bottomless abyss?

Yes, that seems to catch the flavor of it.
The difficulty of living in the moment,
the current calm eye of the storm.

1/29/14

Alok the Doctor

Because you are who you are
you are a trigger.

It helps that you don't wear a white coat
and it helps that you smile and listen and speak

and trust as if we are both smart adults,
which we are.

It helps that you receive
as well as give,

that you are a teacher and a student
as am I.

It helps that you are frank
and open and funny even.

I have come to you
as you have come for me

at precisely this right time.
What will we make of

the lofty trajectory
of the narrative arc

of the ongoing healing story
being written mostly by me?

1/31/14

To Affirm

Whatever comes
I can handle it
I have what I need
to be resilient.

Calm steady strong
the winds won't shake me
or not for long.

2/2/14

At Home in the Universe

I can't remember where I was
when I got lost and so
I wandered more than 40 days
not exactly in the wilderness.

It maybe looked like
going through the normal motions,
but at an unnoticed cost. And now
I can't go back or reclaim.

The only option-choice is forward
and which path. Free-will and all that.
A yellow-brick road appears
and the slippers to click.

Take one step. One small step,
try it or stop and re-choose.
No directions or goals but this:
Remain true and persist.

If discouragement sets in
or its cousin, frustration,
remain true and persist.

If you become trapped
in lofty expectation,
remain true and persist.

Listen to the voices:
You are not homeless
as if there is one place to rest,

but at home in the universe.

2/8/14

Amidst the Buzz
Eric Whitacre at Alice Millar Chapel

"*Do not make yourself small*"
the silent voice said as I sat at the end of the pew

in the chapel where I'd never been…
and very close to you.

I *had* become smaller, to not be noticed perhaps,
familiar feeling I could not trust?

As an experiment I let go of
feeling intimidated.

I uncrossed my arms and breathed
air into my body as if blowing up an inflatable doll.

Could I become myself,
risk being at full strength,

no excuses to fall back on if I failed
in my clearly unstated mission?

Breathe, expand, feel energy flowing,
slowly aura grows, needing nothing.

Breathe and hold the space,
no questions to ask, only listening.

Receive what is offered, no control over anything,
feeling awareness of everything,

holding the space for what was to be, as if
every word spoken by anyone was wisdom passed down

for everyone, including and especially for me.
Give and receive, barriers and barricades demolished,

vulnerable and powerful,
the truth suddenly so obvious.

2/14/14

Ripple Effect
From EW

Writing without looking head on
finding words just outside peripheral vision

Do not turn to minutely examine
for they aren't yet real in this dimension

until caught by someone
and pulled through the veil-lace

Some are urgent advice from the other side
some a healing comfort, some a spectacular wild ride

The vibration they store
is like nothing else here

Some people are ready to receive, some not
nothing you can do about it

2/18/14

Under the Influence
Of acupuncture

If I were a car
which of course I am
a vehicle to travel in
to an unspecified destination

Anyway…if I were a car
of any make or model
at some point I would have
to stop and refuel

And the quantity of fuel
and the quality of fuel
would affect performance
and ultimate distance

How obvious.

2/18/14

Melt

Sun slant on
sheer water veneer
shimmer golden

2/18/14

This Night

Even a half moon
through a hole in the clouds
is enough to throw
down the labyrinth of long shadows

The usual witness
stands in the dark window

2/18/14

Full in It

I am aware spring will come
but I am sitting warm where I am
living a life that picks me up when I get down.

I do not wish to jump ahead and not notice
the sparkle of flakes gently swirling
the quiet freshening after each snowfall.

I am here riding the waves of these days
not struggling against what is.
Perhaps it was the surgery in December

recovery with no expectation of being out in the weather
or maybe this moment right here, right now
is the only one I can feel the possibility of bliss

whatever it is.

2/20/14

Metamorphosis of Water

Now the air
becomes water
as fog swallows
the skeleton trees,
the blue sky dome.

Snow melts to
and through dirt,
layers upon layers
meld back into earth.
Today water flows,

but in the coming cold
becomes solid
and slippery and hard,
some forms reflection,
some potential destruction

and in the end
mostly forgotten.

2/22/14

Empress of Inertia

An object in motion tends
to stay in motion and
an object at rest tends
to stay at rest.

And I—not an object except in physics—
when awake want to stay awake and
when asleep want to stay asleep
so life becomes navigation

of inevitable transitions.
Day into night, night into day
the struggle to stay…
and repeat…and repeat….

2/23/14

West Yard

Slant of sun on
field of snow
highlighting
every wind-dimple
every shallow

overlaid by
stick-tree shadows
dark trunks against
warm orange on sparkle
and mild dirt white

2/24/14

Red Fox

A fox by the woodpile,
red against the split trunks,
pressing down flat looking for holes,
the homes of his next meal.

Plush tail lowered, ears perked,
white front, black boots,
sunny snow-thaw afternoon
headed for another freeze.

2/27/14

Seven Deer at Dusk

Seven deer at dusk in the yard at once
looking for green, not finding much.

Snow had melted under the pines
what grew in the mulch already munched.

Strong and young they are to be sure
not babies, but not elders either.

Some may have been born in spring
delivered onto the flat patch by the back fence.

Now in this severe winter they are
reduced to eating white pine needles

near enough to ground to neck-stretch.
Walking stately through crusted snow

leaving cloven tracks as they go
not much to find to fill a large mammal

no refuge, nor forage nor warmth.
Stop to watch us behind the glass.

2/28/14

Metaphor for What?

I stand on the slope of an active volcano.
I may become embedded in lava, bruised by rocks
buried in ash or poisoned by gas...

or not.

The grumbling giant may sleep again
or I may run or beam up
or die and be re-born
but this crucial moment

of pure potential, of clarity electric
with possibility, this moment
of heightened sensitivity
at the precise balance point

where anything could happen
is exactly the part when I come in
and begin...writing my life
as a conscious act of co-creation.

3/4/14

Sturgeon Bay
Desktop photo

I would like to tell you
I stood on the deck of the wood-slat dock
staring out to a limitless horizon

and my mind calmed with the calm water
and my heart opened with the expansiveness
and the clarity down to rocks on lake bottom

subtly seeped into me.
But no, I am the one standing to the side
with camera in hand, shifting feet

to get just the right desirable slant
of the empty dock with the metal poles
and the metal ladder into cold water

barely dimpled by the wind,
making sure to level the horizon.
Yes, I am in this picture by proxy

to catch and preserve something
that somehow called to me.

3/9/14

Familiar Dark

A long while since
I have seen this
particular darkness.

Slid precipitously down
from some height and
still sliding.

Out of nowhere though
a rationale can be made
piecing together the fragments

of a reasonable pattern.
I was fine as usual
and then it felt

like I was waiting
for a terminal phone call...
just a matter of time

until the end.
Or like a plane had crashed
snuffing out enough lives

to be felt across the earth.
You may be lucky and
not know what I mean or

you may be human and
know exactly.
Did you bring the rescue rope?

A kind word is not enough
to bring back the sense of purpose
I lost from certainty to fog

to this dark deep.
So easily did I assume
I would now glide forever.

***

Not right to leave you there
to worry in the dark with me,
days passed and the boat righted

as it always has.

3/9/14

Another Crisis

You can trust me
now to ask
when I am flailing.

You can see I know
when to let go
when to reach for you.

Not like before when
I would have to be
scraped and bleeding.

Not like before
when I would have to be
sobbing and broken.

Now I know when
I cross that line
even if I don't like it.

I will always want to
take care of problems myself
but now you know

I remember how lucky I am
to have someone to call on:
Ask and it shall be given.

3/10/14

Office Thaw-Fly

I hit the spring-thaw fly
with the looped microfiber duster
and it did not squash, but stunned
and then on the carpet I smashed
the buzzing fly again, stunned again
got a tissue and scooped him up
apologized and flushed.

Normally I am not violent
and if, as I recommended, he had
kept quiet and not dive-bombed me
in my chair at my desk while working late
he would still be breathing (if flies breathe).
Failing that and avoiding starvation
and other deprivation he could have lived
a solitary day or so until inevitable desiccation.

Without long extensive philosophical consideration
I took action.

3/11/14

Routine Checkup

What is there to say
about routine teeth cleaning
the gaping mouth, the drooling

X-rays, checking gums, plaque removal
find someone to be gentle,
recline with deliberately unclenched fists.

A recap of the past 6 months
relevant ups and downs,
hoping for no more bad news.

3/20/14

Learning to Listen

What if cancer is not
the enemy to fight against
to win at any cost, to cure,

but a messenger from the body
delivering an unwelcome message
the result, but not the cause.

What if we learn to listen
before conditions become so dire,
to correct course, modify, restore balance

change what isn't serving us,
small adjustments before
the messenger is at our door?

Even after delivery, it isn't the specter
of death, doom and gloom, but rather
opportunity and possibility

not leading to where we were headed
but to where we now might go.

3/21/14

2% 5-Year Survival Rate
Talked with her today

She was determined to be
in the 2% who lived,

ready and willing and able
to put it all on the table,

allow healing to enter,
allow old crusted debris to leave.

Reshape her physical body
reboot her mind, refresh her spirit.

No matter any resistance,
she discovered her resilience.

Not knowing the length and breadth
of her future, but in all candor

creating one, and in the course
healing all around her.

3/25/14

Someone Posted on *Facebook*

Lawrence Ferlinghetti is 95 today
and I never did send him that poem he inspired
by his inspired reading in Chicago that day
that turned the compass needle sideways and
the streets in the Loop ran in perpendicular directions

no lie
until things settled down out of the long shadows
out back in the sun, back in touch
with the ground and the somewhere blue sky.

I considered sending him the poem
considered writing the back story
even tracked down the San Francisco address
of City Lights Booksellers
but each time I talked myself out of it

intimidated maybe
or not high enough on the crowded list
or waves of life knocking me flat sometimes.
You would think I'd learned after Vonnegut's death,
and Susannah's, how the good ideas, the kindnesses
left undone are the things later that haunt you
not every day, but sometimes.

3/26/14

1980s at a Guess

A blonde, trim young woman
tall, in fire-engine red high heels
matching belt wrapped around her waist
pristine white knit, shoulder-padded dress.

She is dashing across a New York City
street clutching a small red purse
hurrying to a fine restaurant
she has never been to and will not

ever eat at again, with or without her husband.
Of all the moments since then
she is not trapped there exactly,
eternally in the middle of something,

but on her way to and never arriving.
Of all the outfits and trips of a lifetime
how good it felt that specific moment
is what has stuck with me.

3/27/14

Threadbare

There is this thing
that happens sometimes
when I am buoyant
and you are not, and
at the end you are light
and I am left with nothing.

You may not even notice
because I look the same,
but I am face down in the dirt.
If I am angry, as is likely,
for a moment it is at you,
but then as always
the snake turns on me,
fangs bared.

3/27/14

Melt Gift

From the gentle melt
a torn condom
as gift left in the street
in front of our mailbox

its origin unknown
why here, a mystery
as are so many other things
my searching eyes see

3/28/14

In the Dark Mist of the Past

Lone streetlight through the trees
by a road where cars occasionally pass

puddles in a field covered by skim of ice
mud underneath, stamped by small red vinyl boots.

A little girl looks through the glass
of a specific picture window in the country

watching cars whiz by and waits...waits...
for them to come take her home.

Her white-blonde sausage curls
her wide blue eyes and chubby hands

broad smile revealing baby teeth.
She has been sent away, kindly but firmly

to where there is no accommodation for children
away from the life she has known.

Years pass and life plays out
and still as a mature woman sometimes

she looks out a specific window at night
transported back...longing.

3/29/14

Dear Wednesday:

You caused me to think about
my past moving forward and
how I landed where I am.

How my life is not linear,
how I made conscious choices
sometimes from joy, sometimes pain.

We have not met yet but
I woke thinking about possibility
how you stepped outside a boundary,

a preconception I was unaware I had.
I refer to your brilliant thought
to make your own makeup

how much more self-creation
can there be?
I always chose from

what was offered pre-made
giving over that power
along with so many others.

Somehow from a complex beginning
I made it to bliss
as I began imagining

an unlikely but perfect course.
Despite repeated real and potential rejection
I followed the voice that said "Come,"

leaving all the other unlikely paths
not quite right for me,
learning what I could and needed,

not despairing for long.
Finding enough to keep me going
landing on my feet, becoming

trusting and patient and kind,
continually co-creating for myself
a life worth living.

4/1/14

Noticing Owls
On a Tuesday

This much I can say after
traversing the inevitable tunnel,
the layer upon blinding, numbing layers
of darkness, of fog, of grief.

To recognize and embrace light
to do what comes easily,
back to ordinary what was not,
to ride the normal currents
of each day as if
feet were not quicksand sunk.

To notice—both of us—
three owls in night conversation
one a deeper voice in near woods
one lighter, answering from the field
and another across the street
both softer and farther, but responding still
to owl comments of the other two.

Over time we built this potential possibility,
over time we kept on sometimes patiently,
over time healing began and spread
almost inevitably. A sliver at least hopefully.

4/4/14

To Answer a Question Unstated
From talking with Wednesday

If I were to start over now
knowing what I now know

I would listen more
to heart and gut, not live in my head so much.

I would remember what is most important
not easily forget the wisdom I soaked up,

not wait until I fell off the cliff
to make a simple change.

If I were to start over now
I would change nothing

for each choice led to the next path
and mistakes built eventual compassion.

I would be more confident, less anxious
more trusting-patient, less deaf and blind.

I would remember how much I love stories
as I was co-creating my own.

I would be kinder, less harsh-judging,
I would sleep to recharge, not resist rest.

If I were to start over…now…
as I have done before, I would remember…

all…of this.

No advice to offer my hypothetical self,
but to hold to one small thing:

to be true,
aligning all the rest

to who you are,
as you are always becoming.

As you go *out*
be true

as you go *in*
be true.

As best you can
truth as default

and how will you know it?
By the vibrant radiant

shimmering clear buzz
around and through and from you.

4/4/14

Global Reach
Eric Whitacre and Virtual Choir

This is what you did
and no less,
you said (or did without saying
following a dream-wisp):

*Act as if there are no borders,
no boundaries to connection.
Take this music, this equalizer
and sing by yourself with us,*

*all inclusive, all welcome.
If you are inexperienced
or polished or shy or not tech savvy,
if you are new to singing*

*or an old hand at performance,
if you have the will and determination
to follow me, I will lead you.
Where this takes us I do not know.*

This much I know, (you said
without saying) *it is worth the trying.*
Once begun became a life force of its own,
moths irresistibly drawn to your charismatic flame,

not to die in spectacular, if futile, immolation,
but to ride on persistent innovation,
rising above or co-existing with convection
trusting the potent power of co-creation.

One thing leads to another...
and here we are....

4/6/14

Approaching 40 Yrs. Married

There was a time once
when my lips would not leave
your lips and
my breath co-mingled with
your breath and my longing surpassed
anything I had ever felt.

And that was a place to start.
But fire consumes and leaves ash unless
a way is found to transmute the flame
and a foundation is built to sustain
the long-term mutual intention.

Now we are grown different
than we might have been, life companions
the lasting base upon which was built
compassionate support and
common encouragement as each of us in turn
was ground up and spit out by life sometimes,

the outcome uncertain, yet never once alone.

4/7/14

Controlled Burn
Prairie preserve along Riverwoods Road

Smoke as if the whole forest
was in flames, but no,
deliberately set while still damp enough,
a controlled burn of the underbrush,

healthful, part of catastrophic fire
prevention, to clear out under specific
circumstances, the choking old and dead,
and encourage incipient growth.

Fire marshals in yellow gear
stand watch at the perimeter.
Yes, that's what I need:
someone to stand by watching me

as every so often the path and the past
is burned away in constructive conflagration.

4/17/14

Snow In April

The difference between
April and autumn snow
is not moisture content
or frequency or depth
though those may be true,
it is expectation of duration.

Once you hit April you know
any new snow will go in a day or so
followed by imminent warmth
of mild days with increasing light,
buds and blooms and green again
from black and white.

4/20/14

Self-Kindness
For a dear friend (and me)

To let yourself
be yourself
even encourage those aspects
that have been hidden
to come into the sun
even those facets you thought
you could reveal to no one.

To baptize the whole
with kindness
that is enough
you are enough
on your chosen journey
of loving acceptance.
Be gentle and kind *to you* as if

you were someone else.
Remember you cannot give
from your essence
depleting your core strength
but only from your excess.
So practice just this one thing:
self-kindness

to build the reserves
from which you can draw
in service.

Timeline

2009
Blake back from 3 months in SE Asia
Alex graduates from U. of Illinois
IWWG conference at Skidmore College
Extensive home remodeling
Both kids move back home

2010
3rd abdominal hernia repair surgery
To ER, back in hospital with serious complications
Uncle Tom D. dies
Eric Hoffer Award Honorable Mention for *As Easy as Breathing*
IWWG conference at Brown University
Charlie C. dies (uncle)
40th Bishop Gallagher High School Reunion
GR Dodge Poetry Festival in Newark, NJ
Uncle Chuck W. dies
Sister-in-law Barbara, in hospital

2011
Father-in-law dies after slipping on icy driveway
Brother John, in hospital again, not doing well
Publish *Letting Go and New Beginnings*
Mother-in-law passes away
IWWG conference at Yale University
Alex moves to Chicago for graduate school
Hard fall, to ER by ambulance

2012
Submit alto 2 video for Virtual Choir 3, *Water Night*
Long-time neighbor, Steve, dies
Poem is runner-up for Contemporary Amer. Poetry Prize
SPARK mentorship in Chicago
Letting Go and New Beginnings: Global E-Bk. Hon. Mention
Letting Go and New Beginnings: Int'l Book Awards Finalist

Mom passes away after long decline
Brother John, continues to do poorly
Jean McGrew (dear friend and kindred spirit) dies
To ER, I can't breathe
Admitted to hospital with congestive heart failure
Develop heart arrhythmia
Heart shocked three times to keep in normal rhythm
Husband diagnosed with diverticulitis
4th of the sisters diagnosed with cancer
School shooting in Newtown, Conn.
STM slices off tip of finger, to ER

2013
Youngest sister, Dorothy, has mastectomy
Youngest brother, John, dies of MS
Dorothy has stage 4 cancer, starts drugs therapy
Launch re-designed FullBlooming.com
Uncle Tom S. dies after long illness
Echocardiogram (high anxiety)
To ER with heart arrhythmia, returned to normal naturally
Submit alto and tenor videos for Virtual Choir 4
Aunt Aggie dies
Read for *Willow Review* launch (as Illinois featured author)
Friend of my daughter's disappears
To ER with uncontrollable uterine bleeding
Good echocardiogram results (heart stronger)
New gynecological oncology surgeon, Alok Pant, MD
Second surgeon is fatally hit by train
In hospital for hysterectomy
Endometrial cancer is found in uterus after removal
Husband of my good friend, Karen, dies

2014
Frequent follow-up visits with Alok Pant MD
Read poem, "My Own Tribute," for audience before Folkstage
Very severe winter, bitter cold with deep snows
Meet composer, Eric Whitacre, and local Virtual Choir members
40th wedding anniversary

Notes: Poems

About grammar: Each poem is like a small world unto itself. When I write I try to catch the essence of the poem. Sometimes that means very little punctuation, enhancing the feeling of flow. Placement of lines on the page is deliberate, making them easy to read aloud.

Floating On Sitar Notes and Drum Beats
The Peacock is a nearby Indian restaurant. Can you smell the curry and spices and hear the sitar playing, the drum beating in the background?

Put Down the Sword of Self-Wounding
Definitions of immolate: To kill as a sacrifice, to kill (oneself) by fire, to destroy. *The American Heritage Dictionary, 3rd edition, 1992*

Scene: The Future
Refers to my 2007 surgery: bilateral mastectomy and removal of the ovaries (third breast tumor, BRCA 2 mutation) and also my cancer treatment in 1996 (bilateral lumpectomies, chemotherapy, and extensive radiation). See my book, *As Easy as Breathing*, and chapbook, *New Year's Eve Surgery*.

Collagen
Main structural protein found in animal connective tissue (including humans). *New Oxford American Dictionary* on MacBook Pro

Mirror: For Jan Gerber
Jan Gerber is the coordinator and curator of *Women's Journeys in Fiber*, a series of process art projects by Chicago women artists. I read this poem at the artists' reception for *Women's Journey in Fiber Retrospective Exhibit*, November, 2009.

A Way to Release Sorrow
From imagery following a healing session with Tricia Eldridge, founder of the EnergyTouch® School for Advanced Healing.

Soave
Italian: gentle, delicate, soft or smooth. *Dictionary Reverso*.
As a musical term: smoothly, gently. *Wikipedia*

Selective Memory
Beginning refers to multiple sclerosis symptoms that took an integrative approach, including extensive physical rehab, spiritual re-connection and energy work, to restore.

Speaking Kidney
According to Mayo Clinic (online), the human body is about 60% water on average. It varies according to a number of factors including hydration state, gender, age, health and weight.

Post Surgery Follow-Up
Insights following EnergyTouch® healing session with Tricia Eldridge.

Inspired
Folkstage is a series of live performances of folk music on WFMT radio in Chicago, IL, hosted by Rich Warren.

Doors (3)
IWWG is the International Women's Writing Guild. In 2010 the annual conference was at Brown University in Providence, RI.

Dodge Poetry Festival #5
In 2010 the Geraldine R. Dodge Poetry Festival was held in Newark, NJ.

Just Before Tops Diner
The Passaic River runs through Newark, NJ and right outside my hotel window where I stayed for the Dodge Poetry Festival.

Hard Fall
It was Stephen's 60th birthday weekend. A group of us were walking briskly to brunch. I stepped to the side to allow a jogger to pass and my shoe caught on some stones sticking up around a tree in a Chicago sidewalk. I stumbled a few steps, tried to catch myself and fell hard under a car and onto the curb. Went into shock even while trying to be casual about the whole thing. (Immediately took *Arnica montana*, a homeopathic remedy which I carry in my purse.) Led to my first ambulance ride and an ER visit at a nearby hospital. In one of those weird twists, the ER doctor went to school with my son. Eventually turned out I had cracked and bruised the greater tuberosity (part of shoulder), partially torn the rotator cuff, and banged up my knees.

Startling Starlings
Murmuration: Flock of starlings "wheeling and darting through the sky in tight, fluid formations." *The Atlantic,* Feb. 28, 2014

Choosing Expansive
Spark is a volunteer mentor program in a number of cities in the US including Chicago. Through one-on-one apprenticeships they help middle school students in underserved communities improve school attendance and performance as students head on to high school.

Reborn at 60
Perigee moon is at the point in its orbit that is nearest the earth.

Medication
To the ER not able to breathe. Admitted to the hospital with congestive heart failure within weeks of my mother's death (grief-stricken), where I developed an irregular heartbeat (cardiac arrhythmia). My heart required shock therapy to return to normal rhythm. Prescribed medications.

Permission to Myself
Shooting at Sandy Hook Elementary School in Newtown, CT.

Metastases
An image to help healing for my youngest sister, Dorothy, who was diagnosed with aggressive stage 4, breast cancer.

From Jerry de G
Posted on Facebook about an artist who used dew as his medium.

Coming to Terms
Insights from EnergyTouch® healing sessions with Roberta Leenhouts.

Hope and Direction
"Water Night" was originally a choral piece by Eric Whitacre (used for Virtual Choir 3). He later recorded a lush instrumental version on his CD, *Water Night*.

Heart Instructions/Description
At home I woke in the night with rapid and irregular heartbeat (no identifiable reason). Overnight in the hospital normal rhythm returned on its own. I repeated these affirmations to help calm the heart and support good rhythm. I also sang gentle songs aloud (private room), which felt calming. Heart stayed in normal rhythm and I was discharged in the morning.

Antidote to Violence
A singer in Virtual Choir 4, Heidi from Turkey, in the midst of ongoing violence in her city, posted on Facebook this powerful quote by Leonard Bernstein (written upon the death of John F. Kennedy): "This will be our reply to violence: to make music more intensely, more beautifully, more devotedly than ever before."

Virtual Choir 4
Virtual Choir was created by conductor and composer, Eric Whitacre. He makes a video of himself conducting one of his choral pieces and posts the individual musical scores to learn online. Singers all over the world learn the music and individually record their parts, uploading videos which are then assembled into a "virtual choir." VC 4 had 8409 videos from 101 countries. Elisabeth is on the VC support team.

For Kelly's Mom
Kelly Dwyer, a high school friend of my daughter's, disappeared Oct. 11, 2013 in Milwaukee, WI. She is still missing.

Uterus 2
"All of me, why not take all of me?" Popular jazz song from 1931. Words and music by Detroit songwriters, Gerald Marks and Seymour Simons. My voice teacher, Kip Snyder, and I both thought of this line at about the same time regarding my surgeries.

Rewind: Senseless Tragedy
Victor was a young, gifted surgeon I was going to consult about hernia repair. The day before my appointment we got a call he had been in a fatal accident. (It turned out his car was hit by a train as he tried to go around the lowered gate.)

Addendum to the Life List
Refers to my poem: "Life Review of External Scars" (9/4/08) posted on my blog in 2009.

Changing Rules
Facebook news articles: NaCl (sodium chloride, table salt) under pressure makes new forms, previously unseen. Large pyramid under water near islands off Portugal ("stories that could have been told"). Photos by a Russian mother catch the beauty of her young children. Shared with the world.

Vanished
Also about Kelly Dwyer.

Familiar Dark
As it happens, a plane went missing (disappeared from civilian radar) flying from Malaysia to China on 3/8/14 (1:30 AM, Malaysia time). I do not think I had heard about it before I wrote this poem.

Dear Wednesday:
She graduated from the University of Chicago and contacted me about writing.

Notes: Photos

Cover: *Light through Once Molten Glass.* (2013) With sun shining up through it, I took this photo from the top looking through the inside bottom of a glass blown vase made by Jeremy Popelka (Popelka Trenchard Fine Art Glass Gallery, Sturgeon Bay, WI).

2009: *Path to Miami Beach,* FL.

2010: *Winter Roads Unseen,* Lincolnshire, IL.

2010, Surgery: *Up from the John F. Kennedy Memorial,* Dallas, TX.

2010, Life Resumes: *Heading Out,* Chicago O'Hare International Airport, IL. "Sky's the Limit" neon lights installation by Michael Hayden.

2011: *Chicago River Looking out to Navy Pier,* Chicago, IL. Winter night from the 31st floor of the Hyatt Regency Hotel.

2012: *Approaching Loop Intersection,* Chicago, IL. On a trip into Chicago when I was a Spark Mentor.

2013: *Unexpected Wave,* Caught Stephen on a beach north of San Diego, CA (We both got soaked!)

2013, Surgery: *Christmas Lights through Raindrops,* Lincolnshire, IL.

2014: *Gift Embedded,* Sandcast glass with pear inclusion by Stephanie Trenchard (Popelka Trenchard Fine Art Glass Gallery, Sturgeon Bay, WI). Photo taken on my kitchen table.

Author Photo: Margaret Dubay Mikus (2013) taken by Stephen Mikus in San Diego, CA.

End: *Cast Off and Landing* (The end...is also the beginning...) 2013, Sturgeon Bay, WI.

With the exception of the author photo (taken by Stephen Mikus, 2013), all photographs were taken by Margaret Dubay Mikus in the same year as the poems of that section. (Copyrights are the year photo was taken.)

Thrown Again into the Frazzle Machine **is also available as an E-book with full color photographs.**

About the Author

Margaret Dubay Mikus

Growing up in suburbs of Detroit, I was the second of seven children. As the oldest daughter, I had a lot of responsibility for care of the younger kids and we all had household chores. Often I escaped into reading, which opened up new worlds for me. Singing was another joy. Both of these passions shaped my whole life.

I met my future husband on the first day of an English class at the University of Michigan when I was 19. We were married after I graduated with a B.S. in Zoology. We moved to Chicago, a city with opportunities for both of us. I earned a Ph.D. in Microbiology from the University of Chicago, headed for a career in molecular genetics research and teaching.

After a research fellowship, we moved north and I chose to be primary caregiver for our two young children. I also taught biology courses at Lake Forest College. Healing from multiple sclerosis (and then breast cancer a year later) transformed me, cracking open my creativity and redirecting my life. In 1995 I began a poetic journal to "sing from the heart."

I began sharing my poems, which turned out to resonate with others. When I had cancer in 1996, I gave a three-ring binder of about 80 poems to the breast center nurse at a local hospital. She gave copies of the poems to women who were newly diagnosed with cancer.

My healing journey gradually led me to integrate conventional and holistic medicine. At the recommendation of my doctors, I began working with a clinical psychologist who suggested therapeutic massage, which led to healing energy work with several wonderful practitioners over the years. Reiki, Healing Touch, music, psychotherapy, yoga, walks, acupressure, spiritual re-connection, guided imagery, acupuncture, voice lessons, homeopathy, and of course writing, became integral to my healing practice. I read extensively, took workshops, studied, and distilled what worked for me.

I am the mother of two grown, loving children and still married to my college sweetheart. I am strong and healthy in body, mind, emotion, and spirit, a true ongoing accomplishment. My intention is to be fully present each day to an expansive life filled with love and learning, joy and gratitude.

Let's connect! At **www.FullBlooming.com**
and on **Facebook**, **LinkedIn**, and **YouTube**.

The end...is also the beginning...

ALSO BY MARGARET DUBAY MIKUS

Letting Go and New Beginnings: A Mother's Poetic Journey

Global E-Book Award, Honorable Mention (Parenting/Family Non-Fiction)

International Book Awards, Finalist (E-Book Autobiography/Biography/Memoir)

Book of the Month, *Spirit Imprints* magazine, May, 2012

"It's the story of loving and letting go, the bittersweet feeling all parents feel, all people feel when our cherished ones start to move on. I found the poems to be beautiful and timely—mirroring the transition I find myself in now—letting go, new beginnings. I also love how the imagery of the photographs expresses and compliments the intentions of the poems."
Karen Gottlieb

"Margaret's poems are always personal, and yet universal....I highly recommend this book not just to any parent who is at a point where they have to let go of their children, but also to all sensitive readers who are working on letting go in any way."
Pramod Uday, Spiritual teacher from India

As Easy as Breathing: Reclaiming Power for Healing and Transformation—Poems, Letters and Inner Listening

Eric Hoffer Award, Honorable Mention (Self-help/ Spiritual)

"...The author searches for meaning and healing in life's everyday moments.... Unafraid to give voice to her pain, disappointments, doubts and fears, she remains trustingly receptive and hopeful...inspires and uplifts through sensitive, honest, and accessible poetry."
The US Review of Books: The Eric Hoffer Award © 2010
(This quote is used on the front cover.)

"Beautiful book full of the poetry of life"
Bernie Siegel, MD

"[Her] 'from the heart' poems...are true forms of prayer. I believe these poems are truly beautiful and inspiring."
Rev. Ron Roth

"I received As Easy as Breathing *as a gift. What a treasure!...I will read and re-read it for many years to come. Thank you for your insight."*
Linda W.

"Your book is just wonderful!...And now you are helping so many others."
Mikki G., oncology RN

Full Blooming: Selections from a Poetic Journal (CD)

"...listening to this CD is like a deep relaxing session of meditation. You will find your fatigue and stress has been removed and that your soul has been nourished and replenished from within."
Pramod Uday

"Your voice is magnificent! [Your CD] is wonderful! My sister was diagnosed 3 weeks ago with breast cancer and I am going to listen to it with her."
Frani R., healer

"I listen to your CD in the car on long drives. It keeps me peaceful...."
David Buskin, singer/songwriter

www.FullBlooming.com

Praise for the Poetry of Margaret Dubay Mikus

"Her poetry and art work are extraordinary."
Belleruth Naparstek, *author* (on healthjourneys.com)

"From reading 'To Dance Is To Be,' I can see how such inspiring words can give people the power to battle through times of despair."
Lou Conte, *founder of Hubbard Street Dance*

"My classes appreciated your poetry sessions. They have added such a dimension to their views of poetry reading and poetry writing."
Anne B., *seventh grade teacher*

"I am a Lutheran minister who was given a photocopy of your poem 'Cancer Can Give [You]' by a member who died of breast cancer. The poem was read at her memorial service."
Dennis H.K.

"The message of your poetry and experiences was so powerful."
Marci L., *support group coordinator*

"Your poem ['Mantles of Transformation']...expressed exactly what we have all gone through in this process of creation. What a gift."
Jan Gerber, *curator of* Women's Journeys in Fiber

"My daughter is studying poetry and [for an assignment] ended up picking three of your poems [from As Easy as Breathing] *to illustrate how she had learned not to be afraid of change."*
Karen G.

"Stunning simplicity. And Joy." ["From Maya Angelou"]
Margot Van Stuytman, *poet*

www.ingramcontent.com/pod-product-compliance
Lightning Source LLC
Chambersburg PA
CBHW022055150426
43195CB00008B/144